MW01242741

More Precious Than Silver

Living the #ChristianLife in the Digital Age

JOEL BENNETT

WESTBOW
PRESS®
A DIVISION OF THOMAS NELSON
& ZONDERVAN

WestBow Press books may be ordered through booksellers or by contacting:

WestBow Press
A Division of Thomas Nelson & Zondervan
1663 Liberty Drive
Bloomington, IN 47403
www.westbowpress.com
1 (866) 928-1240

ISBN: 978-1-9736-3436-2 (sc)
ISBN: 978-1-9736-3435-5 (hc)
ISBN: 978-1-9736-3437-9 (e)

Library of Congress Control Number: 2018908370

Print information available on the last page.

WestBow Press rev. date: 8/15/2018

To Sam, Savannah, Charlotte, and Violet

Blessed are those who find wisdom, those who gain understanding, for she is more profitable than silver and yields better returns than gold.
—Proverbs 3:13–14

Contents

Introduction

Whether you are just preparing to take flight from the comfort and safety of your parents' watchful eyes, left to flesh out the struggles and responsibilities of adulthood on your own, or if that single gray hair you see in the mirror every day reminds you that there have been a few years since responsibility and accountability were merely abstract words in your vocabulary, there is no better time to pause and take stock of where you have been and where you are going. Regardless of where you find yourself currently, you've no doubt experienced the pain of rejection, the sting of failure, the sourness of a relationship gone bad, or the insecurity that stems from the virtual social world that exists in your pocket. But to make sense of it all and to better prepare for the experiences and expectations that lie ahead requires the right perspective and wisdom that few possess—at least not without the benefit of hindsight.

The circumstances under which you find yourself transitioning from childhood to adulthood are so historically unique that this transition, once so shockingly mundane, now has its own name, *adulting*. The process that took previous generations a few short years to complete can now stretch long into your twenties and thirties. Adulting implies that this process encompasses a significant amount of time where you are not quite a child but not yet an adult. Adulting, the verb, has taken the noun hostage. When you adult, you are carrying out one or two of the responsibilities of adulthood while delaying the hard parts as long as possible.

But to your credit, no generation has ever been more pressed, pressured, and tempted by every passing whim and vice that so easily ensnares us, if only for a brief second. A few seconds is all it takes to derail even the best of plans and intentions. You are being pulled, like a taut rope, between childhood and adulthood, security in Christ and conformity with the world, community and individuality, and the God of the ages and the god of the moment.

And the enemy is not giving up. He'll pull until his hands are burned and calloused with everything in his arsenal. He'll use it all: comparison, bullying, social media, pornography, sex, marriage, and relationships. The greater its capacity for love and goodness, the more likely he is to use it. It's far easier to deceive that way. There isn't a sin in this world that love hasn't justified at one point or another.

These threats and lies have always been around, but never have they been so targeted, so calculated, and so easily consumed and believed. The devices in our pockets continue to change the equation by inviting—unfiltered, unabated, and unsolicited—the thoughts, expressions, and opinions of whatever organization pays the most to put them in front of our faces. It's so easy to be led astray by our own wanderings or the baited hook left dangling in front of us. Older generations, those who grew up without the internet and social media, may be ill-equipped to show you the path to adulthood. Their wisdom was more than enough to see my generation through this transition, but the game has changed greatly, which is why it's now incumbent on my generation, the in-between generation, that grew up alongside this technology before it had the stranglehold on our lives that it does now, to help you navigate your way through it. By our inaction, we leave you to figure it all out on your own. By connecting you to the internet without providing direction or boundaries, we open up a world you are not completely ready for. It's a world that requires a degree of self-discipline and self-censorship that most people simply don't possess, as much as we would like to think that they do.

Of course, it's not just the internet that should give us cause for concern. It has shaped our culture immensely, but more than anything, it has provided an amplifier to the culture of our time. It's a megaphone for whatever ideas or passionate causes our society drums up. But in an era of twenty-four-hour news networks, tweets, Instagram feeds, and fake news, truth has a way of being buried beneath the headlines, the selfies, or 120 impulsive characters and hashtags so deep that it can be a real challenge to dig it out while sifting through the noise.

Along this bumpy path toward maturity, you'll likely be inundated with thoughts of inadequacy at the hands of comparison. You'll see or experience bullying, very likely through the medium of social media where a comment that was meant to belittle or demean was left for all to see. You'll be faced with tough decisions and stiff consequences as we test the boundaries of personal privacy. And you'll struggle, like generations before you, through the mire of sex, marriage, and relationships.

As a parent, I often think about what I want my own children to learn and how I want them to behave when they're older. But all too often, it remains just that, a thought. I may bring voice to these ideas on occasion when sitting down with other parents or my wife (in the rare event that we have the energy to do something other than watch Netflix after the kids go to bed). And I certainly try to act on these ideas as best I can, but sometimes they need to hear these things straight from my mouth. Sure, they'll get bits and pieces here and there, mostly in passing or when they're in trouble and the old "when I was your age" bit comes up. But that rocky passage of time somewhere between high school and that first career can be a tumultuous and haphazard evolution from childhood into adulthood. To navigate it soundly requires clarity of vision and intentional guidance. This is my attempt to provide that vision, perspective, and understanding of the complicated young adult world around you.

CHAPTER 1
Who Are You?

Before you go seeking approval from others and figuring out who you want to be, I'm going to tell you who you already are. All sorts of things are out there screaming at us, trying to convince us that we should look like this or act like that. These voices tell us when we should be offended or excited, what we should buy, or what's acceptable for us to look at. Most of these voices do not come from trustworthy sources. At best, they are misguided. At worst, they are lying to you. Sometimes you need a little help sifting through the voices, quieting the ones that will lead you astray and leave you troubled, empty, or questioning.

To see through all the noise, you need to be looking through the right lens. A lens, as we all know, is just a curved piece of glass that allows light to pass through. It lets in all light without discrimination. But when the light passes through, the lens refracts it. It bends each light wave, directing it to a focal point. In other words, it lets everything in but puts it all into better focus. It doesn't leave it unchanged. It allows you to see everything within its view with clarity. And when you can see things clearly, you can better react to the obstacles in your way.

In aviation, early on in their training, pilots are taught the skills to properly manage their crews and the many resources at their disposal to constantly build their situational awareness. As a pilot flies, she is continuously collecting information from

1

multiple sources: from the instruments, radios, navigational charts, crewmembers, and sensory organs. Each of these bits and pieces of information combines to build a picture of the world around her so she can build her situational awareness. More precisely, situational awareness is defined as how well your perception of the world around you mirrors reality.

When everything is working fine, with each system working in harmony like a symphony of information, flying is no problem, and you can be assured that your perception of your orientation in space and time is true and accurate. But what happens when you take away little pieces of information? What happens when some of that information is missing or wrong? If you take away the sunlight, you are plunged into darkness, losing your most critical sensory organ. Now take away a trusted instrument that decides to quit working at the wrong time. Add to this dozens of voices and calls on the radio, only a small fraction of which are for you, leaving your brain struggling to sift through the noise, waiting, straining, and listening for that key communication directed solely at you.

Suddenly you question what you're seeing outside the cockpit. Are those runway lights? Cars speeding down a highway? Stars? Your body does not know how to react, and you begin to wonder if you're right side up or upside down. Now your situational awareness, your perception of the world around you, is blurred, confused, and wrong. The only way to combat the illusions and misinformation surrounding you on all sides is to build your situational awareness, and the only way it's built is through experience and trust. In these times of confusion, when it's pitch-black outside and the body is disoriented, pilots are taught one thing: to trust their instruments. Yes, even your body will lie to you, telling you you're in a sharp turn when you're really straight and level. Trust your instruments. Forget what your body is telling you. Forget what the world is shouting at you. Focus on the instruments you have in front of you, and ignore everything else.

Information is constantly bombarding teenagers and young adults in this digital age. Sometimes you seek it out, crave it, and devour it. Other times it seeks you out, craves you, and devours you. Before you fly solo, you need to learn what information out there is good and trustworthy, what's bad, and what's just noise. You are developing your own instrument panel right now, whether you realize it or not. Your instruments—all the gauges, dials, and numbers on a screen—give you the facts. These come from your parents, teachers, pastor, church, or trusted friends. Some of these facts will come with experience—of which you have very little. Trust me. In the meantime, you'll need some help filling in the holes.

It's tough to decipher the good from the bad when things are coming at you from all directions, and growing up with tablets, computers, and the internet in your pocket, it is most definitely coming at you from all directions. Your friends at school, television, social media, teachers, professors, parents, movies, and commercials are all competing for your attention. You need help building your situational awareness of the world around you so you can be confident knowing that your perception of the world and your role in it is a good and true representation of reality. So in times of confusion, you can trust your instruments so your perception of *you* better mirrors the reality of who God created you to be.

You Are Strong

I did a little boxing in college. It's a great sport that is both physically and mentally demanding. It requires physical strength, mental toughness, stamina, and a little bit of craziness. I loved it. I loved the competition. I loved facing my opponent one on one. I loved the punishing training that pushed my body to the limit and the reward of landing a solid punch or slipping just beneath my opponent's outstretched arm because I could somehow sense his punch coming. Yes, there was pain. But I wouldn't have had it any other way. Ultimately I loved the testing of my own strength.

When you are pressed, your strength is revealed. You may not believe it, but wait until the punches start flying. Then you'll realize just how strong you are. You may not appear so on the outside, but with every punch, slip, obstacle, and setback, your strength is growing. Somewhere deep inside is a powerful, unique strength ready to make its debut. You may not have abs of steel or see each striation on all four finely tuned muscles in your perfectly sculpted quadriceps, but you are strong. Physical strength is great, and you should always strive to keep your body in good physical condition. It is, after all, the only one you have. But strength is not limited to the amount of weight you can press above your head.

I have a good friend from my time in the navy who struggled through flight school. He is, admittedly, not the brightest tool in the shed. Honestly, his intellect might have been a little behind many of the other pilots around him. It was something he was keenly aware of. He knew it took him much longer than others to grasp difficult concepts or memorize procedures. He was well aware of his weaknesses and shortcomings—so well aware, in fact, that he became determined not to let them get in the way of his goals.

Instead he pushed himself harder than anyone else. He studied harder and longer than most people have the capacity for. He went in to work on weekends to study and prepare for flights. He sought help from people who were a step ahead of him, and he never gave up. When tough jobs that no one else wanted opened up, he'd be the first to volunteer for them. His strength was in his determination. It was in his willingness to work harder than everyone else around him. Lord knows he didn't necessarily possess the natural gifts and talents of most of the other pilots around him, and he took his fair share of ridicule for it.

But his hard work paid off. His leaders and commanding officers took notice of his drive, and when an instructor spot opened up, they chose him to fill it, much to the disbelief of his peers. But his leaders saw what his peers did not. He had outworked them all, and they knew he would carry this strength wherever he went.

Your strength is there. I promise. Maybe, like my friend, you can work harder and longer than anyone else around you. It may be that you have the strength of endurance. You can run farther or faster than most. Perhaps you have the strength of fortitude or grit. You never give up, no matter what the scoreboard says or how far behind you are. It might be the strength of patience. You can outlast anyone without breaking, quietly waiting until everyone else has given up. Maybe you are smarter than all your friends are. You quickly understand the most difficult concepts. Maybe your strength lies in your ability to withstand pain, to stoically bear the stress that causes others to crumble. Whatever it is, you are strong.

Strength comes in many shapes and sizes, but sometimes it needs a little help coming out. It needs to be tested. Don't misunderstand what I'm saying. Too much stress on your body or mind can be damaging. But the right amount of stress will sharpen you, surprise you, and reveal the magnitude of the strength within.

So challenge yourself. Test yourself. Nothing will test you better than a little healthy competition. Face your opponents— man-to-man or woman-to-woman—and leave it all out on the field. And you know what? You'll find that, most of the time, physical strength is no match for mental toughness. You have strength in there somewhere. Find it. Test it. Let it out, and make it stronger. You won't regret it.

You Are Weak

> But he said to me, "My grace is sufficient for you, for my power is made perfect in weakness." Therefore I will boast all the more gladly about my weaknesses, so that Christ's power may rest on me. (2 Corinthians 12:19)

I hate to be the bearer of bad news, but you are also weak. There's just no other way around it. There will be certain things that everyone seems to be better at than you are. Even the friends you have or the people you see who appear to have it all together, who seem to be good at everything, are weak too. There's something even they could use a little help with every now and then.

I have always been very good at not letting the small details slip by. I'm a perfectionist, so I'll carry things out to completion, making sure every step is completed just right—all the i's dotted, t's crossed, and boxes checked—before moving on. But sometimes I have trouble seeing the bigger picture. I have difficulty making decisions with limited information, preferring instead to delay them until I can gather enough data to be persuaded one way or another. Intuition eludes me. Rational objectivity is my solution to ambiguity.

But the world isn't always so accommodating to my strengths. Shades of gray far outweigh the black and white. As a pilot, I can see how these traits both aided and hindered me. The profession matched up well with my detailed nature—following checklists, having a procedure for everything, abiding by clear rules, and using plenty of gauges and instruments that had to fit neatly into a prescribed range. If that were all there was to it, I'd have been set. Any monkey can be trained to fly. Believe me. I trained some of them. But you earn your wings by making decisions. And those decisions are almost always ambiguous.

There were times when I was flying an important mission and something would go wrong, a system that wasn't quite cooperating or weather that was just on the edge of accommodating. Do I continue or turn back? Do I land on the beach or head back to base? I confess. Many times, I'd hope for something to degrade further so my decision would be made for me. For a pilot, that was a huge weakness.

I have another friend who was the exact opposite. I would watch as he would make each decision effortlessly and confidently, without second-guessing himself. It seemed he could step into any problem and arrive at a decisive conclusion within moments. He saw things differently than I did. He flew from his gut, letting his intuition direct his moves. And nine times out of ten, his gut was right. He was comfortable deviating, when necessary, from the procedures. He challenged the status quo, and he always seemed to leave things better than he found them. Me? I'm the reason the status quo exists.

I envied the ease with which he commanded the aircraft and the way he could see problems before anyone else. *Why can't I do that?* I wondered. *Why don't I see things like he does?*

The fact is, my inclination for indecision is a big weakness, one I've known and had to adapt to for quite a while. But weaknesses are not to be feared; nor are they something to be ashamed of. They help us to rely on one another. My friend and I made a great team. Though he often saw the bigger picture before I could even open my eyes, he tended to forget about the details. And when we flew together, I was there to fill them in for him. We relied on one another as leaders, pilots, and friends. We complimented each other. Our strengths covered each other's weaknesses, which made our friendship both unexpected and unshakeable.

The truth is that God made us just the way we are for a reason because His strength is made perfect in weakness. I didn't need to envy the strengths I did not possess. I should have given a nod to my own strengths and realized that my weaknesses were placed in me, just as they are in you, to remind us that we need Him. Just when we think we've built ourselves an impenetrable fortress, God will show us just how foolish and weak we are. It's not to spite us. It's to remind us that we must depend on Him. Our weaknesses keep us humble. They remind us who is really in control. They teach us to rely on others because our God is a relational God and He wants us to lean on Him as well as live in community with others. Don't boast in your strengths. They are a gift to you and are multiplied when you give them freely to others. But be humble, and accept others' strength.

You are weak. Embrace it with a humble spirit. Lean on God, and let His strength be made perfect in you.

You Are Capable

When you were just a toddler, we taught you the most basic things in life: how to feed yourself, stack blocks, and pee somewhere other than your pants. The simple stuff. As you've grown older, we gradually began to introduce the scarier, more complicated things, like how to do the laundry, wash dishes, mow the lawn, and drive a car.

Eventually you will be out of the house and off on your own, ready to face the challenges that are sure to find you. For some kids, this is a very scary thought. For others, you may feel like you were ready ages ago and you can't wait to hit the road. Regardless of whether you're anxious to leave or you plan to delay leaving home until you come home one day to find all your stuff sitting in the driveway, at some point you will be on your own.

I remember when I first graduated from the Naval Academy. I was so excited to finally live on my own. I remember when I moved in to my first apartment how I felt like I was finally a real adult, complete with bills and responsibilities. I pulled up in my Honda Accord that was filled with all my earthly belongings, unloaded the car, blew up my air mattress, unfolded my lawn chairs, and sat in the living room with my roommate.

As we were basking in the glory of our newfound freedom, the sun began to set, and I started to feel something very strange. A slight aching in my stomach had been building throughout the day. I tried to ignore it, to brush it aside as the jitters or the uncertainty that comes during times of transition, but then it finally occurred to me. *I'm hungry*, I thought to myself.

Yep, that's what it was. There was no mess hall, no cafeteria to go to, and no meal plan. My meal plan was me because no one was going to fix anything for me. I was on my own.

Someday you will find yourself on your own, and you'll be faced with a problem you may not know how to handle. Of course, in this day and age, you could easily just pick up the phone and call your wise parents.

And you know what I'll say? "Boy, that does sound like a tough problem. Let me know when you figure it out!"

Okay, I might not say it quite like that, but I'll certainly be thinking it. What I might tell you, though, is, "You are much more capable than you think."

You see, we've already taught you the basics. You remember how to feed and clothe yourself, right? Now it's time for you to figure out that you are capable of learning things on your own because sometimes too much help can be a hindrance. I could hold your hand through every trial and tribulation you face, no matter how small, but that would deprive you of the wonderful sense of pride and confidence you'll gain by doing something especially hard on your own.

I could help you with every algebra problem your teachers throw at you, but all you'd learn is that your father is the best-looking math whiz you've ever seen. (Just ask my wife. She *loves* that about me!) But when I let you struggle on your own, until bit by bit you piece the solution together by yourself, you get smarter. But more importantly, you learn that you can figure it out on your own.

This independence, this understanding that you are a capable person, comes more naturally to some people than others. It's also a lesson that some people will never learn. Perhaps they had parents who were too scared to let them fail or too concerned with making them feel comfortable rather than capable. Maybe they were simply never told—and hence never believed—that they could face the world on their own. They will instead grow up believing that every problem is too difficult for them to handle by themselves.

Not you. This is a lesson that's too important to be overlooked.

There is nothing more satisfying than learning just how capable you are, and there is no better way to learn it than to face a tough problem on your own and survive. Not necessarily succeed, mind you, but survive. Failure is a much better teacher than success.

It is much too easy in this day and age to be dependent. You have the internet at your fingertips. Your parents and friends are just a text or phone call away. It's easy to become dependent and, even easier, as a parent, to enable that behavior in you. It's easy to be overprotective, overly involved, and overly worried. Maybe we want to be needed or want to be sure you are always safe. Surely this is part of it, but I think it is more likely something deeper. We think that more communication, more involvement, more texts, more phone calls, and more of everything makes us closer to you, when in reality, it does two things: it makes you dependent on us, and in so doing, it feeds our own insecurities.

I can feel the angry responses being hurled at me. "But I love my kids! They need me! They call me all the time! I can't just let them struggle! What kind of parent would I be?"

I get the temptation to solve every problem we can for you, our children. But there is strength in the struggle and love in these lessons. Too much help is a hindrance. It enables dependence and prevents you from learning one of the most important lessons of your life. You are capable—much more than you think. You are strong, as you now know, and you have weaknesses too. But your capabilities, once you fully acknowledge them, are limitless.

You Are Beautiful

Before you roll your eyes and skip on to the next chapter, know this. It's as important as it is true. You are beautiful. While I do believe this applies to both girls and boys, I wholly acknowledge that, for some reason, this seems to be a much bigger issue for girls than it is for boys. Read on though, boys. You might learn something. I mean, would it kill you to be a little more sensitive?

There's an incredibly beautiful woman I know named Hannah. Long before I knew her—and way before her children were even a sparkle in her green eyes—she was a beautiful young girl. She loved the outdoors and animals. She'd climb trees, feed cows and chickens, and go for walks in her parents' pasture. Perhaps she was not your typical girl. She was much less inclined to play house or dress-up or get into her mother's makeup than other girls. She was not a "girly girl." (In fact, she would find that notion to be quite offensive to her.) In many respects, she was unlike other girls, save for this. She desperately wanted to feel beautiful. More accurately, she wanted to *hear* that she was beautiful. She *needed* to hear it— and not just from anyone either. She needed to hear it from the most important man in her life, her father.

Why is it so important for girls to hear this from their fathers? The short answer is that I don't know. I have no idea why God created men and women the way He did. But I do know that it is more important than ever that girls hear this from their fathers. Of course, they also need to hear how smart and strong they are and how they can achieve anything they want to in this world. It's just that people don't tend to post pictures of their report cards on Facebook. They don't seem too concerned with the number of likes they get when they give an update on how well they did on their chemistry final.

But when the sun is setting, the background is perfect, the wind is right, your hair and makeup couldn't be any better, and you snap what you consider to be the most perfectly timed, perfectly framed picture where your mole is visible but it's okay because it's in a shadow so you proudly post it for all to see, you better believe every reaction, comment, and like will be tallied and compared. And that one negative comment? It will erase from memory the thousands of accolades that came before it.

We desperately want to feel beautiful. We want to measure up to the beautiful models we see everywhere. We want our friends to acknowledge it. We invite total strangers to comment on it.

But still, even in today's social media-centered world, there is one person whose opinion matters most to girls of all ages. Just like Hannah, girls need to hear from their fathers that they are beautiful.

But for Hannah, here is the sad part. She never did—not as a little girl, not when she paraded through the house in her brand-new Easter dress, not in high school, not when she left for prom, and not even on her wedding day. She has never heard the words "you are beautiful" from the lips of her own father.

It's such a terrible irony that the people who should love you the most, who are entrusted with your care and well-being, whom you have no other choice but to love, can also inflict the most pain and damage. Sometimes the absence of the simplest gesture can cause the deepest wounds.

To be sure, scars remain to this day, marks left not by action but by inaction, as if she were born with valleys waiting to be filled in by loving words from a loving father. Valleys waiting, but never filled.

Words are a powerful thing. They can tear down just as easily as they build up. They can contain healing, love, compassion, and restoration. But sometimes their absence can say more than a thousand words. Don't let an opportunity slip by without saying something.

Here is the good news. I'm saying it right now to you, my dear daughter. You are beautiful. But don't take it from me.

> How beautiful you are, my darling! Oh, how beautiful! (Song of Songs 1:15)

> For you created my inmost being; you knit me together in my mother's womb. I praise you because I am fearfully and wonderfully made; your works are wonderful, I know that full well. (Psalm 139:13–14)

Yet you, Lord, are our Father. We are the clay, you
are the potter; we are all the work of your hand.
(Isaiah 64:8)

There you have it, straight from the mouth of your Father.
You see, you were made in His image, in the beautiful likeness of
God our Father. Not perfect, but perfectly made. A loving Father
fearfully and wonderfully made you, and you are set apart to do
His works.

Have you ever seen the Mona Lisa, the classic work of Leonardo
da Vinci? If you've ever seen a picture of her and look very closely,
you'll notice one thing. She has no eyebrows! This widely accepted
masterpiece, on display in the Louvre in Paris, which one of the
most well-known artists in history painted, lacks the most basic
of facial features. She's a masterpiece—without eyebrows. Did he
make a mistake? Or did she really not have them?

Given the gravity of da Vinci's work, I think it's safe to assume
it was intentional. And that's just it. You can be imperfect and still
be a perfect work of art. In fact, I think it's safe to say that your
imperfections were placed there intentionally. And like the Mona
Lisa, your beauty doesn't stem from perfection, but from every
intentional, purposeful, and unique brushstroke that makes you
who you are, a reflection of the Creator. You are a priceless work
of art, crafted by the potter, for the potter. You are beautiful, and
don't you forget it. Your Father says so.

You Are a Child of God

I have some news for you. You better sit down for this. Are you
ready? Here goes. You were adopted. I'm sorry I didn't tell you before.
I was just waiting for when you were old enough to understand. But
you don't have to be upset. Let me explain.

When you were born, your mother and I were right there,
ready to receive you into this world and wrap you up in a warm

blanket. I was ready to hold you up to my chest and whisper to you in a soft voice. Your mother was ready to cradle you in her arms and hold you gently up to her breast. At that point, she was all the nourishment you needed. And she gave to you freely and happily, proud to be your source of life. Though she had only just met you, she gave to you out of the purest of love.

You were so fortunate to have been born into a family of two loving parents. And did you know that we loved you even before you were born? Long before you came into this world, we lovingly busied ourselves while preparing for your arrival. There was much to be done. You needed a room and a warm bed, a nightlight so you wouldn't wake up scared in the middle of the night, clothes to wear, diapers, and a whole host of things. And then you came, like a miracle, and our months of work and preparation were answered with the cries of a beautiful child.

And now you're older. You are less dependent on us than you once were. You don't need our constant supervision and careful attention anymore. You can reach things on your own now, you eat solid food, and you can finally take yourself to the bathroom.

But you are still our child, born into our family. And yet adopted you are. You see, when you meet Jesus, when you know Him and are known by Him, and when you reciprocate the love He's always had for you, you are adopted into His family. By His grace, He has taken you in as one of His own. He cleans you, clothes you, and provides you with the nourishment that only He is capable of providing and the only nourishment you truly need to receive.

There may be those reading this who may not fully understand this grace. Perhaps you weren't born into a family with two loving parents. Maybe you feel like there hasn't been a single person in your entire life who prepared anything for you, loved you, or provided for you. Perhaps you wished and prayed for a mommy and a daddy to come along, a room of your own, that bed, or those clothes, but you never received them. Maybe you are an orphan, born to no one, expected by no one, and loved by no one.

Well, I have good news for you. Our God specializes in orphans, and He is ready to adopt you into His family. Believe it or not, God loved you before you were even born. In fact, He has been preparing for you this whole time. He's been longing for the day when you finally meet Him and run to Him so He can wrap you up in His arms and whisper to you in His still, soft voice so He can fill you with light to drown out the darkness, feed you through His spirit, and clothe you in light.

So you think you're not good enough for Him? You're right. You aren't. No one—not one—is good enough. This is the miracle of grace. That is, when you accept His love for you and are adopted into His family, you are forgiven, washed clean, and made new. Grace is when you receive what you don't deserve. His love for His children is unconditional, which means His love for *you* is unconditional. After all, you are a child of God.

CHAPTER 2
Social Media, Overconsumption, and the Problem of Instant Everything

> Like a city whose walls are broken through is a person who lacks self-control.
>
> —Proverbs 25:28

I recently deleted Facebook from my phone. I didn't delete my profile entirely (I'm not a monster). But simply removing it from my phone was the first step in acknowledging that maybe I don't need instant access to this time-waster at every moment throughout the day. The first few days without it were somewhat odd. I must have picked up my phone two dozen times throughout the day, unlocked it, swiped left and right a few times, and then set it back down without so much as checking the weather. It's as if it were a completely involuntary action, as natural and mindless as scratching a bug bite on my ankle. I didn't even think about it until the phone was unlocked and in my hands, and I finally noticed that what I was looking for wasn't there anymore.

After a few days of doing this, I thought to myself, *Just how many times a day did I reach for my phone to glance at Facebook? How many hours must I have wasted in short chunks of five minutes, ten minutes, or more? And what in the world did I do while sitting on the toilet before Facebook?*

It's safe to say that you are growing up in a very different world than the one your parents grew up in. You will never know what it was like to go to the bathroom before social media existed. (Thank goodness.) Times were rough in the old days. Let me tell ya.

Since my time growing up sans smartphone, the pace of growth in technology has been staggering. When I was a kid, there were no laptops, tablets, or smartphones. Cell phones weren't even affordable to the masses until I was in high school. I remember when my parents got a "car phone," a big, clunky device that was permanently mounted in the minivan and added an extra antenna to the car. It was pretty cool.

Prior to that, there was no cable TV, which came before Netflix. You had to watch whatever was on at that time and get up from the couch to change the channel because there were only a few different channels, and okay, never mind. All the stuff you have now didn't exist, okay? But at the rate things are going now, I won't even have to teach my children how to drive a car because soon automobiles will be driving themselves.

Technology moves quickly. Along with all the conveniences that technology has brought us comes some serious challenges, those I did not have to face as a kid. They are challenges that, as a society today, we are still trying to figure out. For instance, how can people still feel so alone despite all the connectedness, sharing, and communication that our five thousand Facebook friends affords to you? You are the first generation in history that will grow up from birth to adulthood in a world where online bullying, social media addiction, privacy issues, sexting, pornography, and a host of other radically new and radically available vices are literally at your fingertips.

Other generations had their own challenges, but these are yours. If ever there were a generation that was being set up for a complete meltdown in self-control, this is it. The real kicker is this. While you are learning to struggle your way through this mess, odds are, your parents are too.

There is a good chance you have already struggled with some of these things already, if not all of them. They say you learn best from your own mistakes. This may be true, but it doesn't mean you can't learn from others' mistakes first, thereby saving yourself a slew of heartaches and humiliation. In fact, I'd say that some lessons are best learned through someone else's mistakes. Go ahead. Stick your finger in that socket. Let me know how it goes for you. I don't need to feel that pain for myself when I can clearly see that it shocked the fire out of you. I don't need to do stupid, avoidable things in order to learn for myself that they're stupid and avoidable. I'd rather listen to someone who has been there and done that, whose wisdom and experience exceed that of my own.

You will face many challenges ahead in this selfie-filled world, but there's no need to step into this mess blindly because the consequences of some mistakes are permanent. So listen up, and let's jump into the interweb of knowledge.

Instant Gratification

The world is growing increasingly impatient. Attention spans are shrinking faster than the polar ice caps. Before you know it, there will be nothing left but a bunch of slush floating around in the poles of our brains, bobbing in clumps in a sea of self-indulgence. It will be a calm sea at least, slow, docile ripples drifting along and changing direction on a whim. It doesn't sound so bad really.

We have done it to ourselves. A vast array of content sits waiting to be summoned with a tap of your finger. It's effortless. We've trained the patience right out of ourselves and replaced it with a series of quick highs that last just long enough to leave us wanting more. No longer do we simply consume. We binge. We consume without ceasing for hours and hours on end, continuing to indulge ourselves long after what was beneficial or necessary. We do this for many reasons: We're tired. We deserve it. We use it as a reward or as an escape. But mostly we do it because *it's easy.*

Giving in to our impulses and desires is, quite simply, easier than doing anything else.

And so, day after day, we trade what's best for what's easiest. We trade productivity, challenges, and relational intimacy all for sedentary entertainment. We stay glued to our devices out of fear that we might miss something, and in doing so, we miss what's right in front of us. It's easy. Effortless. The hard part is overcoming. But most things that are easy are hardly worth the effort. So overcome you must.

I have fallen into this trap myself many times. I come home from a busy day at work, tired from too little sleep, and play with the kids for a while. We'll eat dinner and play outside, play tickle monster, or pretend for a while until it's time for a bath. I'll get them cleaned up and ready for bed, and we'll read a few books. And by the time I'm finally able to sneak out of the room undetected, all I want to do is plop down on the couch for a while until someone can pry me off and get me to bed. It seems like it's the only time during the day that my wife and I have to ourselves, free (mostly) from distractions. It's just so easy to waste it. And that's exactly what happens. Kids in bed? Good. What do you want to watch?

Relaxing has never been so easy and encouraged. We never have time to do anything today with our busy schedules, but somehow we manage to watch all twelve seasons of the binge-worthy show de jour in a matter of weeks. We all need time to unwind from a busy day, but at some point, relaxing ceases to be relaxing and becomes laziness.

Most of us are guilty of relaxing every evening for a couple hours. It requires no planning. We simply turn on Netflix and choose from about ten million titles. It's instantaneous. No longer do we have to wait for anything. If you just look around next time you are in a waiting room, you'll see people sitting there with their phones glued to their eyeballs so at least they can be entertained while they wait.

Now we expect everything to be just as fast as the movies we can summon on our phones. Patience is a thing of the past. Instant gratification is here to rescue us from our own creativity. It comes in many forms: instant TV shows, instant movies, instant music, instant games, instant communication, instant photos, instant (uninformed) answers, or instant shopping. You name it.

In an instant, we can consume more than ever before and still be left unsatisfied. It's as though the easier and faster things come, the less satisfying they are. We soon find that all the consumption in the world will not satisfy us, at least not for long and sometimes not at all.

How many times have you scrolled through your social media feed only to feel worse about yourself than before? We weren't meant to be satisfied in these ways. We weren't *made* to be satisfied in these ways. We were made to relate with real, live, physical people, not to be glued to a screen 24-7. We were made to have conversations and share emotions and experiences face-to-face. We were made to be creative and productive and to control the urges of our earthly flesh. This is why we need to overcome.

Overcoming Overconsumption

So how do we resist the temptation to succumb to our every earthly desire? How can we learn to focus our overstimulated minds? It's not easy, which means it's probably worth it. Here are a few hard ways to overcome overconsumption.

Tech Fast

Fasting has never been a popular idea. Voluntary self-denial sounds about as fun as stubbing your pinky toe on a coffee table. But fasting is literally the opposite of giving in to instant gratification, which also means it's the opposite of easy. Though fasting is more commonly used in reference to denying your body food, the idea here is the same. Denying yourself what you want, need, or crave for a period of time cleanses you. It puts things into perspective. It gives you a fresh outlook and reminds us what we really, truly need rather than what we think we need. In short, it helps us sort out and refocus our needs from our wants and desires.

The Bible talks a lot about fasting in a rather matter-of-fact way, as if it were commonplace then. This discipline seems to have fallen by the wayside, but I wonder if we are really missing out on a great spiritual awakening by not fasting regularly.

We recently made a big change in my house. We all but eliminated screen time six days out of the week. Seem extreme? Well, for starters, we barely have time to watch anything anyway for more than a few seconds at a time. But with four kids (including twins who are still in diapers), we found ourselves in desperate need of simplification. Coming home to a houseful of crying babies makes you want to grab the closest screen and thrust it in front of your bigger kids' faces so you can better focus on the crisis of the moment.

"There! Be entertained. And don't bother me right now."

It works ... for a little while at least. But what seems easy in the moment isn't always the best solution. Here's what would happen: The kids would come home, expecting their devices. If they didn't get their devices, temper tantrums would ensue. If they did get them for an hour (which often became two), temper tantrums would ensue when it came time to take them away. When it wasn't time for them, they would ask for them about ten thousand times a day, which gave us the opportunity to tell them no ten thousand times a day. And when we said no, temper tantrums would ensue.

All we really did by letting them have screen time every day was invite unlimited whining, complaining, and pleading, all separated by short, hour-long stretches of distraction. We told them no more times than any parent should and battled tantrum after tantrum.

Though it is counterintuitive, when we settled on limiting screen time to an hour on Saturdays, strange things happened.

Our older children started playing with each other instead of fighting over what to watch. Sometimes they even play outside. It's crazy! When they came to realize we were serious about the Saturday-only thing, which took about two days, the whining stopped. They didn't ask for their devices because they knew they wouldn't get them. When they didn't ask for them, we didn't have to say no. When we didn't have to say no, they stopped having tantrums. When there was nothing to take away from them, we could call them in for dinner, and they would stop playing and come to dinner. Praise Jesus.

My wife and I adhere to this too. Now after putting our children to bed, we do weird things, like talk to each other. We get more sleep because we aren't keeping ourselves up to finish whatever we were watching. Denying ourselves what we want, crave, or think we need is freeing.

Just like my kids, it may take a day or two to turn the focus from what you used to have to what is now available to you. But once you turn that corner, that whiny little three-year-old inside you will vanish. You'll find more value in your relationships (your real ones, not your online ones). You'll rediscover your creativity. Your productivity will increase.

Pick a day or two (or six) and get unplugged. It's like ripping off a Band-Aid. It hurts for a second until you realize you're still alive. Once you've suppressed all the noise, the silence and the clarity it brings will startle you. Unplug the TV over the next long weekend, and turn off your phone if it's too much of a temptation.

But what if there's an emergency and I need to be contacted? Think about that for a second. When was the last time someone called you with an honest-to-goodness emergency? Something that, no kidding, had to be handled immediately and couldn't wait for tomorrow? This feeling of anxiety you get when you are completely disconnected is merely a symptom of our over-connected, overconsuming world, and it's time to let it go. What it really stems from is our *fear of missing out*. What you'll discover, just as I did when I told Facebook it was no longer welcome on my phone, is that you miss absolutely nothing.

Then again, maybe you will miss a few things:

- the ranting opinions of a distant acquaintance
- the perfect selfies that make you feel less than perfect
- the sterile comments left from someone's feel-sorry-for-me post
- the cat memes
- the I-have-the-best-boyfriend-in-the-world posts that you feel obligated to like, even though it makes you throw up a little in your mouth
- more cat memes
- all the creative advertising that gets flung in your face

You'll miss out on all these things, and you won't *miss* them at all. You won't miss them because, when you unplug, disconnect, and power down, you'll find that your greatest resource, time, just became more abundant. But what do you do with all that time once you unplug? I can think of a few things.

- **Be bored.** You may have experienced this once when you literally scrolled to the end of your Facebook feed. But seriously, allow yourself to be bored and to be without entertainment and figure something out. Spend some time in uninterrupted thought. Read a book. (I know a great one!) Go for a run (but leave your headphones at home). Boredom, much like necessity, leads to creativity, productivity, and progress. In this day and age, we rarely experience boredom because we fill the void with screen time. We don't allow ourselves to be bored anymore. Try it and see what happens.

- **Get active.** Go outside. Take a walk. Run. Ride your bike. Do all the things that us bipeds were made to do. It's funny how our minds can become intensely focused when our bodies are engaged. The best thinking and problem solving you will ever experience is when your body is moving, especially when there is a rhythm and a goal. Listen to the cadence of your feet hitting the pavement or the hypnotic whir of your bicycle wheels and the hum of the pedals. The clarity of mind that accompanies a body engaged is why athletes become addicted to their sport. Rock climbers, surfers, and endurance athletes are addicted to the flow they find themselves in day after day. Engaging your body quiets the mind, calms your anxiety, releases you from the prison of your own expectations, and brings clarity and focus to your thoughts. It's great for the body, but even better for the soul. Getting active in solitude can be like medicine for your soul, but being active with a friend can be great too. Some of the best conversations I've had with friends were on hikes, walks, runs, and rides. Sitting down with a friend is great, but standing up is better. A body engaged is a mind focused. So Get up and get moving.

- **Sit down and eat together.** We humans get things backward all the time. Throughout the rush of the day, we tend to eat on our feet and spend time with our loved ones while sitting down on the couch in front of the TV. Resolve to sit down with one another for meals. Take time out of your busy day to slow things down and converse at the dinner table. There is one big caveat here: leave the TV off and your phones somewhere else. The dinner table is a screen-free zone. You will survive for thirty minutes every night without Snapping, Tweeting, or Instagramming. The dinner table is a time to open up with one another and talk about what's going on in your life, not chat with people who aren't even there. Eating is a strangely social thing. People don't like to eat alone, though at the same time many people would prefer to eat by themselves than to eat with strangers. But most people love to share a meal with family and close friends. It's an intimate thing. What do dates consistently involve? Two people eating together, one on one. (A note for my kids: you can date as much as you want when you're old enough to run for president. Dating leads to babies. Remember that.) Eating together around the table as a family is a great way to be intentional about creating a regular family time as well as unplugging for just a few minutes every day. It's a great way to temper our overconsumption. (But not of meat. Meat is delicious.)

- **Create screen-free zones.** My wife and I have never had a TV in our bedroom. It's one of the best decisions we've ever made. As far as I'm concerned, our bedroom is for two things and two things only, and one of them is sleeping! (I'll have more on the other one later.) Joking aside, when I climb into bed, the phone goes away. Sleep is important, and staring at a screen every night while lying in bed will not help you sleep. Don't believe me? Think of it this way: Can you really not sleep without first warming your face with the soft glow of your smartphone, or is it just too easy to pick it up and start scrolling? Or have you just trained yourself to pull it out whenever you're idle? Remember that bit about being bored? Give it a try. Trust me. It's science. Of course, once you're married, there is another great reason to make the bedroom a screen-free zone (Oh stop! We're not to that chapter yet.) Sometimes watching a movie together on a date night can be fun, but watching TV together while lying in bed every night is an intimacy killer. *But we can still have a TV in our room. We just won't watch it every night.* We've already established that we tend to do whatever is easiest because it's easy, so why make it easy for yourself to watch TV in bed? If you don't have a TV in the bedroom, you won't watch it. Period. The only thing worse than watching TV in bed is staring at your phone. At least with the former you are both watching the same thing. With your phone, you can be lying back to back and never uttering a word to one another, never see each other, or never know what the other person is looking at. It kills intimacy. Make the bedroom a screen-free zone for adults and kids alike. Even kids need their sleep.

When we give in time and time again to the promises of instant gratification, we realize that they do not bear fruit. Why? Giving in to our every fleshly desire is the easy way out. It leaves us overweight, undernourished, out of shape, addicted, enslaved to debt, relationally poor, and unfulfilled. When we live like our sole purpose in life is to consume, what we consume ends up consuming us. Overcoming this mind-set is hard and requires a great deal of self-control. It requires being intentional about how you spend your time, what you choose to do, and, more importantly, what you choose *not* to do. It requires the discipline to not only forego the behaviors and desires that do us harm, but to forego even those things that simply do not provide much of a benefit.

Instead learn to love delayed gratification. Learn to overcome temptation, to put down the phone, turn off the TV, to exercise your body and mind, and to spend your time wisely. Instant gratification seldom meets our expectations. Delayed gratification delivers on its promises. It's hard, but like most hard things, it's worth it.

CHAPTER 3
The Comparison Cycle

Give thanks to the Lord, for he is good; His love endures forever.
—Psalm 107:1

I have the worst dog in the world. He has a few positive traits, I guess. He's fiercely loyal. I'll give him that. Just not to me. He's my stepdog honestly, and he's a ten-pound toy poodle named Charlie. My wife got him shortly before we met, which is a fact Charlie never lets me forget. He's loyal to her and her only. He acts as though I've been trespassing on his territory for the last ten years or so. He seems to feel as though his sole purpose in life is to protect my seemingly helpless wife from every other human being on the planet, especially me. Children, neighbors, or vacuum cleaners, it makes no difference to him. She requires constant protection from whomever whenever.

Let me give you an example. Every night when we're getting ready for bed, Charlie sits quietly underneath the far side of the bed, plotting. After my wife climbs into bed, he begins to creep, ever so slowly, under the bed toward my side. Picture him all tensed up, glaring jealously at my bare feet. He's focused like a cheetah stalking a gazelle, but with a slight, uneasy twitch. His eyes start to get a little crazy as his bottom lip quivers uncontrollably until finally he sees me raise one foot off the ground to climb into bed.

At that very moment, every ounce of anxiety and every furry

inch of insecurity sends him darting out from under that bed. And with a shrill half bark, half growl, like a cross between an Indian war cry and the scream of a teenage girl at a pop concert, he throws himself at my foot, nipping impotently as I leap into bed. He never fails. Every. Single. Night. For the last ten years. It's his little reminder to me that he used to occupy that spot in bed when he was just a puppy. Twenty years from now, when his little bones are decomposing in a shoebox in the backyard, I'll probably still be jumping into bed like I'm trying to qualify for the next Summer Olympics, just out of habit.

Sometimes I catch a glimpse of what other people's dogs are like on Facebook. They're always these big, beautiful, purebred masterpieces that have been trained to fetch the paper and brew coffee before their masters ever get out of bed in the morning. They are full of love and acceptance, doting upon their masters with joyful expectations, determined to please and thrilled to be praised. I see clips of dogs that are war heroes, dogs snuggling with little children without care or concern, and dogs that can perform incredible super-canine feats. Then I look at my pitiful stepdog with his judging eyes that bore holes in my heels, and I think to myself, *Why can't I have a real dog?*

Thus, the cycle begins. It's the cycle of comparison, and it ends in discontentment. It goes something like this: comparison, envy, ingratitude, and discontentment.

First, I see a picture or video of someone else's dog. It triggers me to compare my dog with the perfect-looking specimen I see on the screen. I see all the shortcomings in my own dog where there is only strength in the dog pictured. This leads me to envy. I want a dog like that. I want that shiny coat and joyful spirit with its tricks and its obedience.

Next comes ingratitude. I somehow forget any of the funny or joyful experiences I might have had with Charlie. I take whatever good things he's done for me for granted and see only the ankle-biting, tangled mess of fur in the corner.

Finally there's discontentment. I become unhappy with my current situation. I feel anger and sadness at the fact that my friends can have good dogs, but I'm stuck with a bad dog. Bad, bad dog.

What just happened here? There I was, perfectly happy with my life and, at the very least, indifferent to the fact that my dog left something to be desired. But then I decided to waste ten minutes on social media, to step outside my own mundane life and into the ostensibly extraordinary lives of others.

When I took this step, I began to compare the two. Unhappiness was the result. But what changed? Absolutely nothing changed. My life, my circumstances, my dog, and my sore heels were just the same as they were before I started scrolling, back when I was perfectly content. The only thing that changed was my perspective.

Though social media may have many merits, it also seems to be the place where contentment often goes to die. It dies a slow and lonely death, most often at the hands of comparison. The cycle of comparison has always been around, but it has never been so easy to leap headlong into it, close the door, and hit "Spin." In this vast online universe, there is no shortage of things to compare: your profile picture to someone else's, your well-informed opinions to someone else's misguided ideas, your friends, your followers, and your life to theirs.

You must realize that, when you compare your life to everyone else's online lives, you are comparing your normal to their best. You may be dealing with Monday morning while you're looking at everyone else's Saturday night. Think about it. No one scrolls through dozens of selfies, picks the worst one in which her face is all broken out or his sorry excuse for a dog is photobombing him in the background, and posts it for all to see. No, the picture that is chosen is the very best one that captures the person in the best light, perfect smile and all.

I believe most people would be completely happy with their present circumstances if they simply had nothing to compare them to. Would you be happy to get a B on a calculus exam? What if you later found out all your friends got As? Would you still be happy? What if, instead of As, you later found out all your friends got Cs? Would that change how you felt? Objectively, in each scenario above, a B is a B. It's a good grade in a difficult subject. Your situation didn't change, only your perspective. When it comes to social media, we tend to post our As and neglect to mention anything else.

We post pictures of our family's smiling faces on the beach, not the terrible argument that broke out between mile 105 and mile 120 on the never-ending road trip there. We show the fruits of our labor and our high-flying achievements and omit all the deals that landed with a thud. I'm not saying we should all go out and post every miserable failure and shortcoming that happens along the way, though it might make for an interesting experiment. I'm saying you should acknowledge that the perfect representation of your life online, or anyone else's for that matter, is not a true likeness. It is not worthy of comparison.

No one likes to broadcast their failures, but they will proudly display their successes. There's nothing inherently wrong with this. It's completely natural to want others to see you when you're at your best. The problem is that it doesn't quite reflect reality. Those perfect-looking canines I see online? I didn't see the picture of the shoes they chewed up the other day or the fur that's covering their owner's couch. (Charlie doesn't shed. Boom!)

So next time you find yourself caught in the cycle of comparison while scrolling through social media, check your perspective, and remember that what you're really doing is comparing your Monday morning to someone else's Saturday night.

Comparison is certainly not limited to social media. At school, at work, or even in the car, you can find plenty of people who have what you want. Maybe you see a girl at school every day with a perfectly proportioned body, a smile that exudes confidence, and flowing hair that you're certain looks perfect the minute she gets out of bed. But what you're really seeing when you look at her are your own skinny legs or your own eyes that are too far apart. Perhaps you see someone else's beautiful girlfriend and are reminded of last Saturday night, which you spent at home by yourself.

You see the guy who plays three sports, but the last time you touched a ball was when one smacked you in the face when you weren't looking. (At least that's what you told your friends.) There is no end to comparison or to wishing you were smarter, faster, skinnier, prettier, or stronger than the person across from you.

If I'm completely honest with myself, I'd say that I don't generally struggle with comparison in this way. For me, the cycle of comparison looks a little different. Mine goes something like this: comparison, judgment, ingratitude, and pride. The result is no less sinful and much holier than thou. The outcome here may even be worse than mere discontentment.

It too rears its ugly head while I scroll through the noise, manifesting itself in little voices in my head, saying things like, *What's he trying to make up for with that picture? Does she know how silly that makes her look? Why would you post something so dumb?*

Or while I drive down the street and see someone with a nicer car than mine, those little voices say, *What a stupid thing to spend money on. He's probably in debt up to his eyeballs!* Or if I see someone driving a beater compared to mine, they say, *Clearly he doesn't know how to take care of his car. If he just knew how to save his money, maybe he could buy something nicer, like mine.* There is just no end.

Pride is such a good liar. He'll whisper in your ear, saying he's just confidence and it's okay to be a little confident every now and then, right? His haughtiness finds a way to slip in to almost any situation or comparison and manipulate it into superiority. He's a fault-finder, a judgment-maker, a one-upper. He builds you up at the expense of everyone else. He compels you not just to share your posts online but to compete with them because everyone should know how much better or successful you are and how much harder you work than them. God has a lot to say to those of us who are prideful:

- "When Pride comes, then comes disgrace, but with humility comes wisdom" (Proverbs 11:2).
- "The Lord detests all the proud of heart. Be sure of this: They will not go unpunished" (Proverbs 16:5).
- "Pride goes before destruction, a haughty spirit before a fall" (Proverbs 16:18).

Yikes! Looks like I have some work to do. I have yet to find a verse that says, "The Lord detests all the *discontented* of heart." I'm fairly certain it doesn't exist. I've found plenty of verses that appear to provide comfort to the discontented, but comfort to the proud? I don't think so. What's terrible is that, even as I write this, knowing full well God's stance on pride, pride is still whispering to me as I compare my cycle of comparison (pride) to others' discontentment.

"It could be worse," he says. "You could be over there with all those weak-minded, discontented souls who wallow in their own self-pity on the other side of the cycle."

Yes, that's me. Forgive me.

If you are like me, the Bible provides a clear game plan and a warning. First, the game plan:

- "May I never boast except in the cross of our Lord Jesus Christ, through which the world has been crucified to me, and I to the world" (Galatians 6:14).
- "Do nothing out of selfish ambition or vain conceit. Rather, in humility value others above yourselves" (Philippians 2:3).

Boast only in Jesus. Value others above yourself. It's a recipe for humility, one that should be followed daily by the likes of the proud of heart. It's so simple and yet so hard. But the message of pride is clear, and the outcome is certain. "The greatest among you will be your servant. For those who exalt themselves will be humbled, and those who humble themselves will be exalted" (Matthew 23:11–12). Humble yourself or be humbled. Either way, in the end, pride won't stand.

Ending the Cycle

You may have noticed that both cycles of comparison have one thing in common, ingratitude. It's a little easier to see with discontentment, but that's because pride has a way of spinning things his way. When I compare my car to someone else's car, gratitude is lacking.

I'm not saying, "Oh, I'm so grateful for the reliable car I have instead of that guy's beater" or "Oh, I'm so glad my car is paid for because that guy *must* be making payments on his."

I omit gratitude entirely. I leap from judgment to pride, like one might leap from envy to discontentment. I compare the two and make a judgment, and no matter the result, arrogance overtakes me. Ingratitude is more of an omission than it is an active step, an omission of gratitude. Ingratitude is nothing more than refusing to acknowledge that God is the source from which all blessings flow. Ingratitude paves the way for pride to remove God, allowing you to take full credit and claim superiority for your high position. Or it paves the way for discontentment to reign supreme, disparaging the God whose blessings are never enough. If comparison is the match, then ingratitude is the fuel it ignites within us.

Here's the tricky part: comparison is unavoidable. You can't stop yourself from comparing circumstances, appearances, and the like. Our minds can seldom be kept from going there. It's like those games you see in children's magazines that ask you to find all the differences between two nearly identical pictures. You are drawn to the differences. You are drawn to what sets them apart. No, you cannot defeat the cycle of comparison by avoiding comparison all together. You defeat it with gratitude.

Whether comparison compels you toward pride or discontentment, gratitude is the weapon for which comparison has no defense. Gratitude breaks the cycle, disarming comparison and rendering it useless. But it takes an active and intentional step. When you recognize the gentle tug of envy or the whisper of judgment, that's when the cycle can be broken. You know what follows these is either discontentment or pride, but only if you allow gratitude to be omitted. If you are intentional about inserting gratitude, the cycle cannot continue.

When you start to compare your less-than-perfect body to the pictures you see strewn on the internet and start to wish that your legs, stomach, or hair looked more like hers, stop and be thankful for the body God has given you. It may not be perfect, but surely there is something you can find about it that you love. I can assure you there is something there to be thankful for.

If you are grateful for the healthy body that God has given you, it is much harder to be envious of someone else's. If you are grateful for your job that provides for your family, recognizing that God is your ultimate provider, it is much harder to be prideful for your success. Be grateful, not ashamed, of the lessons failure has taught you. They've given you experience that lends itself to wisdom. Be grateful for the challenges you've faced. They have sharpened your gifts and produced in you perseverance and character. Be grateful for the people God has placed in your life to lead, push, guide, carry, challenge, and encourage you because it is not the number of friends you have that counts. It's the depth of your relationships that matters.

When you step back and reflect on what God has blessed you with, how can you be unhappy? How can you boast, except in Jesus? Every challenge, every relationship, every talent, and every good and perfect gift is from the God who created you, and when you live your life with gratitude, contentment is sure to follow.

So next time my stepdog nips at my feet as I'm climbing back into bed at three o'clock in the morning after putting a crying baby back to sleep, at least I can be thankful that he's been a loyal companion to my wife all these years; he's comforted her and protected her through my deployments; he somehow loves me, despite his odd and eccentric ways; and he's only a dog, and his poor little days are numbered. Oh, come on! I'm not perfect!

CHAPTER 4
Bullying

> Speak up for those who cannot speak for
> themselves, for the rights of all who are destitute.
> Speak up, and judge fairly; defend the rights of the
> poor and needy.
>
> —Proverbs 31:8–9

Bullying has been around since the dawn of man, and yet it has
never been a bigger problem in our culture than it is today. Why
is this? Is it because kids are meaner and less empathetic than
in generations past? Or is it that kids are more sensitive and
more easily offended than they used to be? Perhaps there is some
evidence to suggest the latter. Being offended is now considered
an intramural sport on many college campuses. However, I don't
think this is the biggest reason for the problem. I believe that the
catalyst for the present epidemic known as modern-day bullying
bears more resemblance to the difficult-to-overcome problem of
instant gratification. It's just easy.

Bullying today is easier now than it ever has been before.
At one time, bullies were depicted as the big, angry kids on the
playground who picked and shoved the smaller kids around just
because they could. The classic bully looks a lot like Biff in the 1985
movie *Back to the Future*. Biff was the big, aggressive high school
kid who shoved around George McFly, who might best be described

as a wimp. Biff would intimidate his smaller, weaker classmate into doing his homework for him and giving him money. He thrived on physically and verbally abusing the lesser George, threatening him face-to-face and commanding his respect and obedience. And George? He would just stand there and take it. What else could he do? Biff was much bigger than he was. His classmates knew Biff for striking fear into those he could push around. It was no secret who he was. He was a bully, a moniker he seemed to wear with pride.

Though his bullying ways seemed to withstand the test of time in *Back to the Future*, Biff's time has come and gone. Now bullies can be faceless, nameless shadows sitting behind a computer screen. No longer limited by strength or size, they are protected by anonymity and physical separation and are once removed from the damage they cause. They need not tower over their victims face-to-face or look them in the eye. The blows they deliver are no longer physical, but the pain they inflict is just as real. Their punches are invisible, and the scars, though deep, fall beneath the skin, which is why the damage they cause is so dangerous and debilitating. The protection the internet affords them, the wall of separation put up while the barriers of size and strength are removed, means it has never been easier to launch verbal and psychological assaults.

It's so easy, in fact, that anyone can do it. Today anyone can be a bully—boy, girl, big, small, anyone. Though Biff was known to all his classmates, today bullies can hide in plain sight. Perhaps the only thing known about them is their Twitter handle. They can remain completely anonymous, a fact that affords courage to the cowardly.

Are kids these days less empathetic? No, I don't think so. They just seldom see the effects of their handiwork with their own eyes. One hurtful, impulsive comment left on someone else's account is all it takes. But the aggressor won't even see that blow land. He or she won't see the tears or the sleepless nights. Sure, bullies may see their victims at school the next day, if they even know or are known by them at all, but emotional scars are easily hidden. How easy is it to share and understand another person's feelings when you don't even know him or her, don't see the person, or can't physically see this individual's very real and very human response to a hurtful comment?

The problem is not that kids are less empathetic. The problem is that social media has somehow usurped thousands of years of human interaction, leaving a whole generation struggling to perceive the subtle cues evolution has taught us to pick up on that invoke in us a human, emotional response. When texting, tweeting, or posting, we don't see the physical reaction of our counterpart. We don't see eyebrows raise, lips part, eyes widen, or jaws clench. You don't hear their voice get higher, quivering with emotion. Things get misinterpreted, auto-corrected, and lost in translation. Sarcasm and tongue-in-cheek quips can easily get taken far too seriously or out of context.

Though a Biff-like insult may cause the aggressor to briefly feel clever, self-righteous, or vindicated, he may not even know how deep his comment might have cut. It might give you a quick high after a snarky comment gets a few likes (instant gratification), but without those pesky feelings of guilt that come from witnessing the human effect that might accompany a comment made fact-to-face. Empathy, therefore, eludes you.

Are kids these days more sensitive than they used to be? Maybe. Maybe not. But before you judge someone for being too sensitive, first consider the ramifications of that online comment or picture that is posted or circulated from the victim's perspective. That stuff is permanent. A physical blow or a face-to-face comment? It's here today and gone tomorrow. But once an embarrassing picture or hurtful words hit the internet, they are there in cyberspace forever. And each time you read those words or see that embarrassing photo, you feel that blow again and again and again. The humiliation is compounded many times over. Harsh words carelessly thrown in your face or overheard will hurt, and rumors may spread fast, but an online rumor can literally stretch across the world in milliseconds.

When I was in the navy, about once a year, an email would go viral for all the wrong reasons. I remember one of them vividly. A fellow pilot, unknown to me at the time (but soon known to pretty much every pilot in the navy), was getting out of the navy and applying for jobs from some prominent companies. Upon being rejected for one of these jobs, he wrote back a vindictive and very unprofessional email to the manager who rejected him.

Little did he know, that manager, a former naval officer, still had many friends in the service. He forwarded his email to a dozen leaders, both within the navy and at other similar companies. Each recipient forwarded it on to dozens more with the same question: would you hire a guy like this? Within hours, those words that were so foolishly penned following his rejection for one silly job opening had spanned the globe.

By the time they reached my inbox, thousands and thousands of people had viewed them. I saw email addresses in the chain of emails from Africa, Europe, and bases all over the United States. Now that's embarrassing.

While this was a good lesson in what not to do (and very entertaining to read), it also highlights a particularly troubling aspect of online bullying. Not only is the pain permanent, it is public. There is no hiding it. Once an image is out there, it's there for all to see. Before the birth of the internet, an embarrassing moment might only have been witnessed by a few people who happened to be there at the time. This is no longer. If that same moment is captured in ones and zeros, it can be shared, emailed, tweeted, posted, and/or texted to the point where thousands or even millions may see it. There is no humiliation quite like public humiliation.

Foolishness will always be exposed for what it really is, but let's change the story a little bit. Let's say a girl writes a little note to a very dear and trusted friend at school. Perhaps it's about a guy she likes on the baseball team. Because, of course, the note was meant for one person's eyes only, it's filled with some pretty private and personal thoughts and feelings of the kind you wouldn't want just anyone to know. And let's say her friend carelessly leaves the note out on her desk just long enough for a boy to realize the personal nature of it, pull out his phone, and snap a quick picture of it. He texts the picture of the note to a couple of his friends, and they text it to a couple of theirs. Before you know it, the entire baseball team, as well as the majority of the high school, has seen the note, and those very personal thoughts are now very public.

How mortifying would this be if you were that girl? How completely devastating would it be to know that your personal feelings were no longer personal? How could you go to school each day knowing that everyone you passed in the hall had read your intimate thoughts? Sure, things like this could have happened before the internet, but technology has made it so much easier and faster than ever before. As a result, the degree and frequency with which things like this happen has increased dramatically, making it that much easier for the bullies of the world, big or small, to proliferate their poison.

We all know how much worse this little example could be. But the point is that bullying today is much easier than it was in your parent's generation. The Biffs of the world are just as likely to become victims of bullying today as they are provocateurs. While bullying has gotten easier, the internet has made empathy more elusive than ever. It has enabled the effects of bullying to be both permanent and public. And finally, there is no pain quite like emotional pain. It is the easiest to hide and the hardest to deal with, a perilous combination. So if you think bullying isn't a problem, that it's no different today than it was in generations past or that kids today are just too sensitive, think again.

How to Deal with Bullying

How then do we combat this modern-day affliction? Is it simply unavoidable in this day and age? It is a difficult task to undertake, but you can do a few things to make the online world a little less Biff and a little more Marty McFly.

- **Don't be a bully.** Like I mentioned before, it is so easy these days to become a bully that anyone can do it. Forget what you used to think about bullies, and imagine this: cute little cheerleaders, straight-A students, super nerds, jocks, and video gamers. All have the ability to log in to their social media platform of choice and leave an anonymous (or not so anonymous) trail of binary destruction. Step one is to stop the hemorrhaging. You are the first line of defense against bullying. Use your words and your online presence to build others up, not tear them down. Be a blessing to others while setting the example for your friends and followers. Don't make private matters public, as is so easy to do on social media, not your own and certainly not others. If you feel someone has wronged you, never respond publicly in anger over a private matter. In fact, never respond in anger, period. Cool down first. Then under a less clouded, hormone-filled mind, air your grievances to your offender in person. Or if the thought of confronting conflict face-to-face makes you so anxious you'd rather throw up, write an old-fashioned letter, pen, paper, and all. (But watch your words carefully. Would you be okay with someone else reading it?) Above all else, flee from the temptation to be mean to others.

- **Walk a mile in someone else's selfie.** You may be tempted someday to be mean to someone simply because it's cool or because he or she is an easy target. Maybe there's a kid at school who everyone makes fun of and can't seem to do anything right. Perhaps he's so annoying you just can't stand him or she's so weird that no one wants to be her friend. If you're feeling tempted to poke fun of someone like this in order to fit in, first you should probably question the company you keep. Next, make a deliberate attempt at empathizing with that difficult-to-understand individual. Think to yourself, *What if everyone were spreading rumors about me, talking about me, and making fun of me? How would that make me feel if I were the butt of all their jokes? What if everyone knew my secrets? What if everyone thought they knew my secrets but actually didn't know me at all?* Make a dedicated effort to understand what someone else might be going through and why you think it would feel good to put someone else down. It might help to know that, in my house, if I ever discover one of my perfect children has been bullying someone, online or elsewhere, his phone, tablet, computer, hologram machine, virtual reality system, and anything else they haven't invented yet will become my phone, tablet, and/or computer. After that, we will get in the car and drive to whoever's house he felt was worthy of his disrespect. Then my child will apologize to this person and his or her parents face-to-face before returning home to his disconnected room where he will age slowly, not to emerge until he is old enough to run for president. That is how seriously this issue should be taken.

- **Stand up and fight.** Passivity never changed the world. In *Back to the Future*, George McFly is the epitome of passivity. It is painful to watch him cowering from Biff, accepting as truth the fact that he's helpless against him or that he's not good enough, tough enough, or big enough to be his own man. Marty, George's future son, cannot stand to watch his young father get pushed around in the past. He can't and won't accept this injustice. Marty stands up to the bully, even though he's smaller than the towering Biff, and fights him. What's more, he empowers the wimpy George to eventually stand up for himself.

You may not be a victim, but chances are, you've witnessed one. The world is waiting for someone like you to intervene, to confront injustice, and to stand up for righteousness.

We live in a world that is gravely lacking in love and understanding, where being singled out for race, color, gender, or any number of differences is far too common. And social media has become the platform of choice for the bullies of the world to spread slander and hate. And those bullies look just like you and me. So before you post it, tweet it, or say it, keep this in mind, "But I tell you that everyone will have to give account on the day of judgment for every empty word they have spoken. For by your words you will be acquitted, and by your words you will be condemned" (Matthew 12:36–37).

Your words will have an impact that will far outlast you. In fact, they will have an eternal impact. Choose them wisely, and use them to build up, encourage, and motivate one another in love. There will always be bullies. Your first and best line of defense against bullying is to stand against it yourself.

CHAPTER 5
Privacy: Protect Your Selfie

> But everything exposed by the light becomes visible—and everything that is illuminated becomes a light.
>
> —Ephesians 5:13

My brother and his wife had three children in three years. They just popped them out, one after another, as if they were racing down the aisles on Black Friday, tossing babies in their basket as fast as they could before rushing to the checkout counter. But they are young and good looking and full of energy, so I guess they can do that.

Following this baby "hat trick," my sister-in-law started hitting the gym hard, determined to get her body back into her pre-baby shape. She dieted and exercised, cutting out carbs, added sugar, starch, dairy, gluten, sweets, and most of the things that are generally considered to be food. Instead she ate things with weird-sounding names like legumes, ghee, and vegetables, whatever those are. She counted calories while she counted burpees and squats, all the while counting the pounds as they melted away. Oh, she also documented this whole journey on Instagram, complete with before and after pictures.

I don't have Instagram. It's filled with too many people with perfect bodies who count calories and eat ghee. There's no place for that in my life. I like real food. But she started getting many followers who were impressed by her weight loss progress (though she didn't have much weight to lose in the first place, if you ask me) and wanted to know how she did it. They were genuinely interested in legumes and ghee. These are not my people.

Not long after my sister-in-law reached her weight-loss goal, a friend of hers on Facebook sent her a post. It was one of those click-bait advertisements that had scrolled across her news feed with a catchy headline, like "Stanford grad student discovers magical weight-loss secret." Below the headline were two side-by-side pictures of this young, nicely photoshopped, hip-looking grad student. You've probably seen a million advertisements just like it. The startling thing was that the model in the picture wasn't a Stanford graduate student at all. It was my sister-in-law.

Talk about creepy. Someone out there in cyberspace had come across her Instagram posts, copied her pictures, touched them up, and photoshopped them into an ad. There is no privacy on the internet. But I suppose it could have been a lot worse.

Thus far, I've touched on a few issues that most of us can relate to or at least have some understanding of. But the issue of privacy is a subtle one, with far-reaching and tremendous implications. I intend only to skim the surface and provide some perspective into the importance of keeping vigorous control over the information you post online so your face doesn't end up somewhere it shouldn't. And when I say information, I am not just talking about things like your name, birthday, address, or credit card number (or maybe your dad's credit card number). I'm talking about things like pictures, which can show the whole world where you are or were, where you live, what your hobbies are, who your friends are, where you go to school, where you hang out, and about a million other things. Seeing your picture end up in an advertisement without your knowledge or consent is creepy and unnerving, but it merely scratches the surface of what's possible.

When I was a teenager, before I would hop into my 1989 Isuzu pickup on a Saturday night to go hang out with my friends, my mother would always say, "Be careful. Remember, everyone out there is drunk." What she meant was there are a bunch of idiots out there just waiting to chug a few beers, get in their car, and plow me over at the next traffic light, so watch out for them!

Today, it's more likely that you'll get sideswiped by someone texting while driving rather than by someone drinking and driving. However, in this day and age, I might change her warning slightly. Before any of my children get behind their computers or phones, I would say, "Be careful. Remember, everyone out there wants to follow you on Instagram, stalk you, track you down, kidnap you, and put you in the next *Taken* movie."

Perhaps this is a bit extreme, but unfortunately it is much easier today for predators to attack. They are out there, and without trying to sound too paranoid, you do need to be careful and protect yourself from the creeps, pedophiles, deviants, and others with malicious intent. Call me crazy, but to pretend the problem doesn't exist is just plain naïve. The boogeyman is real, and he has a Facebook account.

Protecting yourself from the scum of the internet takes a little forethought and a lot of common sense. Aside from erasing your online life entirely, tossing your iPhone in a lake, and fashioning a little hat out of aluminum foil, there are a few good ways to protect yourself by simply checking your privacy settings on your social media platform of choice. Most of us gloss over these when we first sign up, never to think of them again. But the time for ignoring these settings is over. Thankfully, it's never too late to dive back in and become familiar with them.

There are settings you can tweak so that things you like, follow, post, and share are only visible to those you want them to be visible to. Check the setting that says something like "who can view my posts" and ensure it doesn't say "public," which means that anyone can see your posts. "Public" might as well say "troll bait." Don't make it easy for those creeps, or someday you're likely to see a picture of yourself advertising some nefarious website.

You can also control who can send you friend requests. Instead of letting just anyone send you a request, enable the setting where only friends of your friends can send you friend requests. If you're like me, you don't like rejecting people.

When I get a random friend request, I'll think, *Do I know this guy? Hmm. I must know him because clearly he knows me.* And then I accept it because I don't want him to think I might have forgotten that the two of us actually met. This is ridiculous. Reject away. You don't want some rando looking at your profile. And chances are, you already have plenty of friends. Who needs one more? When you can only be friended by friends of people you already know, it will significantly limit the number of random friend requests you receive and thus limit the number of people you should reject.

The same goes for the email address and phone number you may have provided to set up an account. Make sure only friends can look you up with this information. Avoid providing any of this information to begin with, if you can help it.

Here's a good one. Googling someone's name can immediately provide a wealth of information about him or her, perhaps much more than is desirable. Often the first thing to pop up when you Google someone's name is his or her Facebook profile. If you don't want your Facebook profile to immediately pop up when someone Googles your name, there is a setting for that. You can find a setting that says something along the lines of, "Do you want search engines (Google) to link to your profile?" No, you don't.

There's a whole host of other settings you can lock down as well. Here's a quick rundown:

- You can control who can post stuff to your page/timeline. (Hint: Only your friends should be able to do this.)
- If you are "tagged" in someone else's post, you can review it before it lands on your timeline.

- You can control who can see posts and photos you've been tagged in. (Again, set this to only friends. But you can also set this to "only me" for extra privacy.)
- You can consider turning off "location settings." Cyber creeps do not need to know where you are all the time.
- You can control who can "follow" your online activity. (Again, set this to only friends.)

Your phone has some settings you can tweak as well. Think no one can tell where you took that cool sunset shot? Think again. Unless you've disabled the geolocation option on your phone's camera, the precise date, time, and GPS location data are embedded directly in the image file. Think about that before you text that cute selfie to the guy you just met the other day, and consider disabling this function in your phone's settings.

These are the basics, but I suggest you become familiar with the privacy settings of your favorite social media apps before you go diving into the deep end. It's also a good idea to revisit these every now and then because social media platforms are constantly evolving and changing them. If you haven't touched them since you signed up, it's time to take another look. But remember this: even the most rigorous privacy settings can't protect you from stupidity. When you let those ones and zeros go, do not think for a moment that you are ever going to get them back.

Don't want anyone but your closest friends to see that picture or comment? Then don't send it. Not in a text, not in a post, not in a house, not with a mouse. Once you go digital, you can never go back. Not only will that go a long way in keeping the predators at bay, it'll help you avoid those pesky cyberbullies as well.

There are other great reasons to pay attention to your online profile as well. When you apply for that first job, you can be sure a social media check has become standard. Be sure that whatever you post isn't something that would disqualify you from that position or is otherwise something you wouldn't want your future boss to see. The same goes for future dates as well, that is, when you're old enough to date (or run for president). That hunky dude or foxy dame you just met is probably racing home right now to friend you. Will this person like what he or she sees?

Remember your audience. In the social media world, that is anyone and everyone. Don't post it unless you're okay if your friends see it, their friends see it, your crush, ex, the person you can't stand, teachers, coaches, or Sunday school teacher sees it. Who am I missing? Oh yeah! Your parents! Because *I will* see it. In fact, that's a great rule of thumb if you are considering whether or not to go live with that post. Ask yourself, *Am I okay with my parents seeing this?*

If the answer is no, then it's safe to say that you probably shouldn't post it. It's easy to think that what you post online will be just as temporary as the quick high you felt while doing it. It's much harder to wrap your mind around the permanence of such actions and the cascade of lasting effects that might stem from them.

I recently read that Harvard withdrew acceptance from ten potential students due to the offensive nature of some of their online activity. Think about that for a second. You've worked hard for years, pounding out essay after essay, staying up late to finish that calculus assignment, and doing all you can to make it to the top of your class. All that work finally pays off as you earn acceptance into one of the most prestigious universities in the world. Think of the nervousness of receiving that letter in the mail that holds your future in the balance, the excitement of opening it, and the relief and joy of discovering the acceptance letter it holds. They want you. You made the cut.

Next comes paperwork and preparation. You are invited to join the Class of 2023 Official Facebook page, where you can join the community of students you will meet in the fall. Now imagine a few of these prospective students ask you to join their "private" message group.

A few weeks later, you receive another letter, but this time it says, "We regret to inform you that, due to the offensive nature of your recent online activity, you will no longer be attending Harvard in the fall."

It happened. Right or wrong, it happened. "Private" apparently only means "private until someone decides to make it public." You can debate about the limits and legality of free speech all you want while you are attending your backup school.

Taming your tongue is no easy task. And just like pictures, protecting your privacy involves taking a careful inventory of the words you post as well. "The tongue is also a fire, a world of evil among the parts of the body. It corrupts the whole body, sets the whole course of one's life on fire, and is itself set on fire by hell" (James 3:6).

It has always been difficult to keep a good hold on your tongue, and it hasn't gotten any easier now that social media has given you an audience for your once-private thoughts. For some reason, when it comes to social media, we say things we would never utter to someone in person. Social media is the stiff drink that lowers our inhibitions, dulls our wits, slurs our speech, and impairs our judgment. It's completely unfiltered. It's easy to lose control, succumb to the deluge of impropriety, and find ourselves diving headlong into matters that should have never even garnered our attention. Those careless words you post will never go away, so you'd better make sure you give them some careful thought before hitting that button, lest they come back to haunt you.

Infrequent and Reserved

Social media is a tool, a release, or an outlet for projecting who you want to be to the world. But acceptance into this world comes at a very stiff price. These platforms are far more powerful than their creators ever imagined, and users should proceed with caution. This should be your mantra when it comes to social media use,

"Infrequent and reserved." Use it, but don't let it take you over. Use it sparingly, and make sure you are spending more time on your physical relationship than on your online ones. When you make a comment or post, temper your language. Hold back a little rather than imbibing to the point of inebriation and letting loose your unfettered tongue. It's too easy to think that the comment you leave will only be read by its intended audience. Don't be fooled by the mirage of privacy because we all know that nothing is truly private online.

CHAPTER 6
Relationships: Walt Disney, God, and Why
Pretty Much Everything You've Heard Isn't True

Come near to God and he will come near to you.
—James 4:8

Finally, we made it to my favorite topic. Relationships are the best. At least relationships are the best when they're not the worst. Relationships of the romantic variety are no stranger to pop culture. Many a song, book, and movie have been written to try to make sense of the complicated world of relationships. I'm willing to bet that more words have been written on this subject than any other in history. Men have always (unsuccessfully) sought to understand women and opined openly about this struggle, and women have always wondered and complained why men don't seem to understand them at all. It's a rich subject that has entertained millions throughout history. But remember, for every happily ever after, there are a dozen Greek tragedies. The former is a myth (sorry), and the latter is completely avoidable.

Misinformation abounds in this messy arena. There is no shortage of people who stand ready to offer you their unsolicited, ill-informed, and misguided advice on relationships. Dysfunction is practically the norm today. It's downright acceptable. Well, it's not acceptable to me, and it shouldn't be to you either. So when your friend, who happens to have a different boyfriend every week and regularly calls you crying because he did this or she said that, wants to offer you relationship advice, listen carefully, thank her for the advice, and proceed to discard her words in the giant dumpster of broken relationships. In short, everyone will spring to offer you advice, but consider the source before you give it the credit, or discredit, it deserves.

I remember a baseball game I played in my senior year of high school. I was playing center field on a beautiful spring day. The batter stepped up to the plate and swung hard at a fastball. I heard the ping of the aluminum bat contacting the ball and saw it fly very high in the air. It took me just a fraction of a second to gauge that its trajectory would carry it short of my position. I began to sprint toward the infield. With every step, I felt like I was falling further behind the gravity that was working so hard against me, pulling the ball faster and faster back toward the earth. I glanced forward to see if the second baseman still had it. He had lost it. Racing full speed, I knew I could still catch it. As it came hurling down, I dove, arm outstretched, and watched the ball land firmly in my glove as my body went sliding into the infield. It was a beautiful catch (if I do say so myself), but it didn't happen by chance.

In practice, the coach would hit us monster fly balls, and I would take off for them. If I determined that I couldn't catch one, I would slow down and watch the ball hit the ground, fielding it on the hop. After all, it's better to slow down and keep the ball in front of you than to go racing for a ball you can't catch, miss it, and have it roll all the way to the fence. But at some point, I decided I *could* catch those balls, but not by staying on my feet. If I were going to make those catches, I was going to have to dive for them, which meant I needed to disregard the self-preserving nature of my body.

So I made a deliberate decision in practice. The next time I didn't think I could make it to that ball before it hit the ground, I would make a dive for it. It was practice, after all, so what did

I have to lose? Failure would cost me nothing. So in practice, that's what I started doing. I didn't make that diving catch during that game because of talent or chance. I made it because that's how I practiced, and the decision to practice that way was a deliberate one.

Diving headers, game-winning catches in the end zone, or out-of-the-park home runs, none of these spectacular plays simply happens by chance. Each of these highlight-reel worthy plays and the athletes who perform them have years behind them of careful study, discipline, and practice. But it's not simply the time spent practicing that matters. If you practice the wrong way to throw a ball, it doesn't matter how much work you put into it. You'll always lose out to someone with the proper coaching. Practice isn't enough. You must practice for success.

Good plays don't just happen, so why do we expect good relationships to? We know that, whether it be sports, public speaking, school, jobs, or any type of competition, as we practice we learn, we grow, and we get better. But as a society, when it comes to relationships, it's like we just throw a bunch of stuff against the wall and see what sticks. I've seen people casually jump from relationship to relationship, throwing themselves blindly into each one and accumulating piles of baggage along the way. People think that, if they can just find that perfect person who fits them just right, then everything will work out on its own.

Make no mistake. You are practicing right now. When you drift from person to person, searching for happiness, fulfillment, or that fairy-tale connection, you are practicing. When you stick it out in a bad or abusive relationship, hoping he or she will change, you are practicing. When you spend your young adulthood practicing all the wrong things, whether it's because you never had a good example of what a healthy relationship looks like, because you've been listening to the wrong people, or because you've been chasing your own physical or emotional gratification, whatever the reason, you should expect your marriage to be no different.

It's time we redefine what a successful relationship looks like. It's time to set some realistic goals instead of believing the fairy tales. It's time we start practicing for a healthy, fulfilling marriage instead of practicing for regret, dysfunction, and divorce. There is nothing better than a good relationship and nothing worse than a bad one.

The One

I enjoy a good Disney movie. They are clever, creative, and filled with wonder and adventure. They make us laugh, smile, and even cry sometimes, if you're the sensitive type. (Not me though.) They are fun to enjoy, but we must not forget that they are fairy tales, not real depictions of how relationships truly play out. If they were, here are some lessons you could take from a collaboration of Disney movies:

- Love at first sight is pretty much the norm.
- Falling in love just kind of happens.
- Weddings should be over-the-top parties.
- Being in love is the only thing that matters.
- Love can see you through any challenge.
- After you get married, you will live happily ever after.
- You'll only be happy if you find *the one*.

These all sound great but have little to do with reality. In fact, it seems like these movies always end at the beginning: the princess marries Prince Charming. All too often, it seems that young adults are working hard to *get* married instead of working hard *to be* married. Of course, you have to get married before you can have a good marriage, but working toward getting married is like sprinting for the starting line instead of preparing for the race that follows. It's no mystery as to why this occurs. We grow up seeing movie after movie that glorifies the search for love and ends at the beginning with the perfect, expensive, fairy-tale wedding. If they kept going, maybe you'd get a chance to see a more realistic depiction of the happily ever after these characters claim to attain.

Take *The Little Mermaid*, for instance. What does that relationship look like a year or two after the movie ends? I can imagine a few things:

> Prince: "We can't go visit your parents this Christmas, Ariel."
>
> Ariel: "Why not? We see your family every Christmas! How's that fair?"
>
> Prince: "Because I'm not a mermaid! We've been over this! I can't go under the sea!"
>
> Ariel: "But it's really beautiful down there. It's way more beautiful than it is here. I really think you'd like it."
>
> Prince: "If I hear one more word about how beautiful it is under the sea, I swear ... Why can't you just be happy here? You chose to have legs and live here with me!"
>
> Ariel: "Well, that was before I knew we'd practically be living with your parents!"

Now there's a movie I'd go see.

These fairy tales are not completely useless. They seem to spend the majority of their time depicting what it's like to be in love, and in that regard, they do a good job capturing what that emotion feels like. When you're in love, it *feels* like you will live happily ever after. It *feels* like you can overcome any obstacle together. It *feels* like there is nothing that love can't conquer, nothing that can get in your way, and nothing that will ever stop you from feeling this way toward the object of your romantic affection.

That gooey, fluttery, heart-melting depiction of love's beginning is a good one. And it's true and honest. At least in that moment it is.

But then the movie ends before we realize that this feeling, as it turns out, doesn't last. The movie ends before the exciting, passionate newness of the chase wears off. They leave us wanting to believe that, if we find *the one*, it just goes on forever. Happily. Ever. After.

The fact is that relationships are much messier and more complicated than they appear in the movies. I'm not bashing Disney by any means. I just think that too many people buy into the fairy tales.

Don't think so? Consider this all-too-common belief passed around in Christian circles. I've heard it many times. It goes something like this: God has the *perfect* person set aside for you. Don't worry because, even though you may not know him or her yet, God is preparing that person *just for you*. And someday, when you're both ready, God will place that one, special person in your life.

Where did this myth come from? Not the Bible, that's for sure. I haven't found anything in there that even remotely comes close to this. If it didn't come from the Bible, where did it originate? Well, it sounds a lot like a Disney movie, doesn't it? It's like Disney meets God. How pleasantly unbiblical.

I have news for you. There is no *the one*. There is not just one single person out there capable of making you happy. In fact, there are probably many people out there with whom you could forge a successful relationship with. If there were only one, what if you missed him or her? What if you made a stupid mistake and married the wrong person? Are you destined to live out a long, unhappy marriage? What if the person God has so carefully prepared for you forgets to look both ways and gets hit by a bus? Are you then doomed to walk the earth hopelessly alone for the rest of your life? No, because there is no *the one*. That is foolishness that stems from a culture that idolizes the chase and can't tell fact from fiction.

Pursue the One

> My heart says of you, "seek his face!" Your face, lord, I will seek. (Psalm 27:8)

If there is no *the one*, then it follows that marriage is a choice: you *choose* to spend your life with someone else. Many people out there could be *the one*. Instead of asking how you find *the one*, maybe you should be asking how to find the *right one*. But before you concern yourself with finding the *right one*, you need to pursue *The One* who is the only one who can fulfill all your needs. Instead of searching for love, pursue the one who is love. Pursue the one who already knows you, loves you, and created you. If you draw near to Him, He will draw near to you. Pursue the one who tells you who you are, who fashioned you in His image, and who called you according to His own purpose.

Pursue the one who feeds you and nourishes your spirit with the bread of life that will never leave you hungry. Pursue the one who fills you with living water. He should be your first love and the only one in whom your joy will be made complete. This is the relationship you should pursue first. Do not worry about tomorrow. Do not worry about finding the perfect man or woman for you. Pursue God. If you grow your relationship with Him, He will show you what's truly important. He is—and should always be—your priority, your primary relationship. Your spouse, your children, your parents, and your friends all fall somewhere behind. When your relationship with God is strong, your relationship with people will be put more clearly into perspective.

This is not news. You've likely heard this before, and that's because our Christian culture thankfully gets this right. You likely already know how you should be pursuing God. But if you don't, ask yourself, "How do I grow closer to the ones I love? How do I kindle the relationships I have with my family and friends?"

Start by spending time with them. It's no different with God. Each and every day, take some time to set aside the distractions of the world and be by yourself. Put away your phone. Sit down in a quiet and secluded place, open your Bible, and start reading. Pick a reading plan if you want, and stick to it. Commit to reading it every day. But don't just read. Take notes, highlight, and really think about the words of the text. Ask questions. Write about your thoughts in a journal, if that's your thing.

There is no better way to grow in your relationship with God than to spend time with Him, and when you sit down to read the Bible, you'll learn who God is. Just like a friend, you'll learn what is important to Him, what makes Him smile, and what makes Him proud. You'll discover what breaks His heart. You will discover what He's done for you and what He has promised you. You'll discover who God is and who He wants you to be.

Of course, when you spend time with a good friend, you'll often find yourself talking a lot. So after reading, talk to Him. Spend time in prayer. First, thank Him for the wonderful blessings in your life. Everyone has things he or she can be thankful for. Perhaps you can thank Him for the people He's placed in your life: your parents, brothers and sisters, teachers, and friends. Thank Him for your health. Thank Him for the challenges in your life that will make you stronger. Whatever you do, begin with a grateful heart.

Next, ask Him for forgiveness. We all fall short each and every day. Not one of us is perfect, so when you ask for forgiveness, be specific, and with humility, search your heart. There's no need to be self-deprecating. Just be honest. Ask Him for help with the struggles and vices that may be uniquely yours. No sin is too great to separate us from our loving Father. Just as your own father will always love you no matter what you do, even more so will your heavenly Father.

Finally, present your requests to God. No request is too small or too big. Just ask. If He's God, you may ask, "Doesn't He already know the needs and desires of my heart?" Yes. But I think He wants us to ask Him anyway. There is power in the asking. There is surrender in the asking. There is acknowledgement of His divine power, our weakness, and His mercy and grace. There is acknowledgement in the asking that He is greater and the only one able to provide for your every need. Most importantly, there is acknowledgment in the asking that He is in control, that He is *The One*. And that is both humbling and empowering.

So yes, search for *The One* with all your heart, mind, soul, and strength, and know that, when you search for Him, you will find Him.

God as Father

> I will proclaim the Lord's decree: He said to me,
> "you are my son; Today I have become your father."
> (Psalm 2:7)

I'm going to go off script here for just a moment. Some of you may have read the lines above about how God will always love you, just like your earthly father, and felt completely bewildered. Maybe that totally missed the target for you because what needs to be acknowledged is this. Not everyone has a good father. You may be completely unable to relate to a god personified as a father. For some of you, the comparison may fill you with rage because your own father was anything but loving, present, or encouraging. Maybe the father you know was not slow to anger or quick to forgive. Maybe you had a stepfather who felt that his role was to remind you every night, in his own special way, that you were not his child. Maybe your real father didn't stick around or had his own

63

demons to fight. You may even be offended by the very notion of God as a Father because that word *father* floods you with pain.

Whether by distance, absence, neglect, abuse, or whatever reason, your earthly father simply didn't know how to love you. And because of that, perhaps now you are unsure how to love. After all, you never had a good role model to show you. Perhaps you are wary now of all the adult men who stumble their way into your life. You are unable to trust because you couldn't rely on the very person you should have been able to rely on the most.

We live in a generation with far too many absent fathers, where single mothers are ubiquitous. For some reason, it seems like the wounds inflicted by fathers tend to go far deeper than any such wounds left behind by mothers. While I won't pretend to understand the asymmetry behind this observation, it is worth acknowledging the heavy responsibility of fatherhood and the resulting heavy consequences of failure.

So if you are offended by the notion of God as Father, I get it. I don't share your experiences, but I acknowledge the fullness of their impact. In Christian circles, we often refer to God as Father and specifically use the masculine pronoun "He." But God is God, no matter what you call Him, and we are *all* made in His image, both men and women.

A beautiful illustration of this is in the book, *The Shack*, by Wm. Paul Young, where God manifests Himself (or Herself) to the protagonist as a large, black woman. I absolutely love this image. I can just imagine being wrapped up in the big, loving embrace of this jolly woman. If this resonates with you too, I won't be offended. Like I said, God is God. He goes beyond gender. But I think the father moniker goes beyond the mere trappings of a patriarchal society. I think God, in His wisdom, knew the impact fathers would have in their children's lives. I'd like to think that, rather than we humans projecting our image of a father onto God, it is God who is projecting His image onto fathers. It's His illustration to a broken world of what a father should look like. It is we who should resemble Him and not the other way around.

So if you can, I would ask that you accept God as the father you never had. He is a good Father who loves without ceasing, who knows how to give good gifts to His children, and who is ever-present and worthy of your faith and trust. He will not leave or reject you, but He will guide and strengthen you in all goodness as He carries out His plan and His purpose through you.

Fairy-Tale Jesus

Let's get back to the fairy tale that says you will one day find *the one* person who will magically complete you, as if you were a sock lost in the dryer and you only have one perfect match. She's tumbling around in there somewhere, waiting for that perfect moment when fate will bring you both together at last by the lint collector. Of course, until then, you will stop at every beautiful, sweet-smelling sock that you see, pair yourself up with it, and try with every fiber to make it a perfect match. Let me be clear about something. You may find a match, but it will never be perfect.

There is great comfort in the myth that fairy-tale Jesus will place your perfect match in your life when the time is right. It absolves you of all responsibility. As is so often believed, when you find *the one*, it will be so perfect and so pure that loving him or her will require no effort whatsoever. It will just work! As long as you're a Christian and your future spouse is a Christian, that's all you need in order to live happily ever after. Never mind that you are not perfect. Forget that your spouse won't be perfect either. But wait? If you're not perfect and your spouse isn't perfect, then how will two imperfect people become perfect when joined together? I'm a math guy, so this is how I see this relationship:

imperfect person + imperfect person ≠ perfect relationship

There you have it, proof that fairy-tale Jesus belongs in his case on the shelf somewhere between *Cinderella* and *The Lion King*.

It will just work. What a rosy, idealistic, and dangerous fallacy that isn't worth the paper it's printed on. Yes, falling in love requires very little effort. But the kind of love that solid marriages are built on, the kind of love that Paul talks about in 1 Corinthians 13, that kind of love takes effort—a great deal of effort. It doesn't just work. It never just works. The type of person that hangs on to that philosophy is the type of person that will go through relationship after relationship, using up the other person like a used car until it no longer meets his or her needs. Once the seats get torn, the shocks give out, and the miles no longer race by like they used to, it's time to trade it in.

When love that came so easily meets the bumpy side of life, when it begins to require effort, those who bought in to the fairy-tale Jesus myth are left stuttering at the realization that their happily ever after looks quite a bit different than what they had imagined. Amidst the struggle, they begin to wonder if they made the right decision, if God's hand was really in it, if their partner really is *the one*.

If fairy-tale Jesus is more than just a figment of your imagination and if God really is just a big matchmaker in the sky, then judging by divorce rates (even among Christians), we have to conclude that perhaps He's not very good at this task. Maybe it's just His hobby, not His full-time gig. Perhaps it's what He tinkers with, you know, when He's in His shop on cool summer evenings.

Before you string me up for heresy, you must know by now that I don't really believe this. If there is even a hint of truth to the fairy-tale matchmaker Jesus myth, then the only reasonable explanation for our pitiful performance after meeting *the one* is us. We mess it up. But if our performance post-marriage, post *the one*, leaves something to be desired, clearly finding *the one* is not even enough to keep us together, negating any magic behind that perfect person. This realization sends us reeling back to the conclusion that there is no *the one* after all.

Oh, but maybe we aren't listening to God. Perhaps in our haste to get married, we stop short of *the one*, settling instead for someone less than perfect, less than what God has planned for us. Of all the excuses, this one probably holds the most water and may even be true in some cases.

But let's assume that's me. What if, in my own selfish impatience, I foolishly married someone who was not the person God had set aside for me? That means my *the one* is still out there somewhere and her *the one* is already spoken for, which would lead her to marry someone who wasn't her *the one*. And then his *the one* would be out of luck. And so on and so forth until the cycle was messed up for everyone. One act of disobedience on my part derails the entire system for everyone.

If marriage is truly important to God, would He allow one person to ruin His plans for everyone else? If marriage is truly important to God, would He allow marriages to fall apart simply because of one act of disobedience? The answer, of course, is no.

This doesn't mean that God's hand is not in marriage. Far from it. If you've been reading this in hopeless angst, do not despair. Reason for despair exists in thinking that there is only one person out there for you in a sea of more than seven billion people. Now that's intimidating. But if you've gotten to this point without tossing this book aside in frustration, know that, as surely as there's no fairy-tale Jesus waiting to betroth you to the one person He has set aside for you, God is present in your struggle to share your life with someone special.

We know that we have a God who delights in giving good gifts to His children. Rather than fashioning one special person to complement each one of us, I think God provides us with opportunities. Rather than being predestined to marry a match God has set aside for us, I think He gives us free will to choose when and with whom we are to enter into that covenant.

But it's almost irrelevant. Wherever you end up, whether you are paired with someone who fits you like a pair of designer skinny jeans or find yourself in a relationship that makes you feel like you are a square peg being forced into a round hole, how you got there is not terribly important. What matters is that you are there. And once you're there, there is work to be done, a spouse to love, and a covenant to uphold.

You may be asking, "What's the difference between a God who has prepared someone especially for me and a God who simply provides me opportunities?"

Let me explain. Let's say you have this perfect job in mind for yourself following school. You've worked hard all through college, building up your résumé, and you finally land an interview for your dream job at your dream company. You know it's going to be the perfect fit. You show up for the interview, and it's as if your whole life has been preparing you for this one moment. Your confidence is met a few days later with a phone call, a job offer, and a salary that far exceeds your expectations. You have arrived. It's as if God designed this job especially for you.

So you go to work. The weeks go by and turn into months and eventually years. You start off working with passion and purpose, and your labor is met with promotions and raises. You put in nights and weekends when you need to because you secretly love it and wouldn't have it any other way.

But a few years go by, and your responsibilities begin to mount. You wake up one morning and think to yourself, *Boy, I'd really rather not go to work today.* And suddenly your perfect job begins to feel a lot like work.

Now when you go to work, you find yourself staring at your watch, eagerly waiting for five o'clock to roll around. Your passion turns into passivity, and your excitement turns into indifference until one day you decide you've had about enough. Instead of working, you arrive at your desk an hour late, stare at Instagram for an hour, grab some coffee, do the absolute minimum needed to get by, and grab some lunch, followed by another hour of Instagram before you finally head home early.

What happens when you decide to stop working? You get fired from your not-so-perfect job. It doesn't matter how many years you worked there or how much of a superstar you were before. When you stop working, you are no longer of use to the company.

Was it really the perfect job? Or was it simply the opportunity you'd been praying for? Or was it that your heart was ready and in the right place to see God's opportunities in front of you clearly as the gifts that they are? You could have excelled in any number of jobs (though not *every* job, of course). If it feels perfect, it likely won't stay that way for long. And regardless of the career you choose to pursue, one thing is certain: the day you stop working is the day your career starts dying.

Opportunities come and go. You may have even let one or two of them slip by you. But just like a good job, I believe you will recognize a good relationship when your heart is in the right place and you can see it for the beautiful opportunity that it is. No, it won't be perfect. All relationships come with trade-offs, though some will certainly fit you better than others do. Every good paycheck comes with long hours, and every good relationship comes with sacrifice. But even the most perfect relationship in the world starts dying the day you stop working for it.

Become the One

> I have hidden your word in my heart that I might
> not sin against you. (Psalm 119:11)

Whether fairy-tale Jesus exists or not, instead of diving headlong into relationship after relationship, searching for that perfect someone, why not try something different? Try to be the person God wants you to be. Would your hypothetical perfect person be happy if she knew what you did on Friday nights? If he knew the habits you'd formed and the things you did when no one was looking? If the answer is no, then you have work to do.

Be the one. That means that you are a work in progress, not a finished product. It means you still have time to change into the person that God has called you to be. Far too many times, I've seen people define themselves not by who they are but by who they're with. Their self-esteem is found in their boyfriends or girlfriends. They collapse under the overwhelming pressure to be liked, so much so that they become slaves to what other people think of them.

Are you a slave to others' perceptions of you? Are you filled with anxiety about the mere thought of not fitting in? Do you feel like you *have* to have the right clothes, the right brands, or the right phone for your friends to accept you? Do you find yourself doing things you don't like to do with your boyfriend or girlfriend just because you want him or her to like you? Do you laugh at things you don't think are funny or feign excitement about things you think are dumb? When you cannot do what you want to do for fear of the judgment of others, you become a slave to them.

This is serious business, so let me say it again. The people you are with do not define you. Your boyfriend or girlfriend does not give you your identity. If your desire for the approval of others causes you to participate in behaviors that you shouldn't be participating in, it means that you are more concerned with the approval of others than with the approval of God. If you let someone else define your identity, it means you care more about what others think of you than who God says you are.

Be the one God has called you to be, and don't forget who you are. You are strong and capable. You are made perfect in weakness. You are a beautiful child of God. Where there is doubt, let this revelation fill you with confidence. Where there is insecurity, trust that your identity and your self-worth are found not in someone else but in God, who fearfully and wonderfully made you in His own image. He did not call you to be a slave to the approval of others. He called you to His own purpose, to love and be loved by Him. Rest in the knowledge that peace and fulfillment comes from no one else but through Him.

Don't worry about tomorrow. Pursue God, and as you pursue Him, allow Him to transform you into the one He has in mind for you to be.

CHAPTER 7
Be Single!

There is a time for everything, and a season for
every activity under the heavens.

—Ecclesiastes 3:1

I can feel your disdainful stares now. Some of you will not like this
chapter. Others of you are saying to yourselves, "Uh, I've already
got this down" and will want to skip to the next chapter. Don't
skip it. And for those of you who can't fathom a weekend without
a date, perhaps you should reread the last chapter and then come
back to this one.

There's a book out there called *I Kissed Dating Goodbye*,
which was popular when I was in high school in the late 1990s.
(I know, weird.) I never read it. My older brother read it, and
shortly thereafter, he began dating a girl who quickly became his
girlfriend, then his fiancée, then his wife, and ultimately his ex-
wife. Ugh.

Needless to say that book is still not very high on my list of
books to read. I'm sure it's fine and all, and I gathered the concept
from those who did read it, but I was never really the dating type
anyway. Sure, I had a girlfriend here and there, and by that, I mean
I had like, two. That's pretty much it. Nothing serious. I'd like to
think I would have had more if it were not for my overwhelming
masculinity, which apparently some girls find intimidating.

I spent most of my high school and college days planted firmly in the single camp. No, I didn't sit at home every Saturday night feeling sorry for myself. In fact, it was quite the opposite. Aside from being able to look at my handsome self in the mirror every day and say, "You heartbreaker, you," being single also gave me the freedom to jump in my car and go hang out with my friends at the drop of a hat. I didn't kiss dating goodbye. I didn't vow only to court girls who could potentially be marriage material. But I also didn't spend my weekends wringing my hands, anxiously lamenting my present circumstances. Though there is plenty to learn through dating, I can say with confidence that those long periods of singleness during high school and college gave me the clarity to see what I truly wanted in a relationship.

Singleness matters. Singleness is important. It's not something to be dreaded or ashamed of. Rather it's critical to becoming that confident person you want to be, whose identity is rooted firmly in Christ, not in the person sitting next to you in the movie theater. Many people may disagree with me on the merits of singlehood. That's fine. Everyone has the right to be wrong. But bear with me as I make my case.

First, let me be clear on what I'm not saying. I'm not saying you should be single your entire life. For most of us, that would be impractical. Living a life alone, holed up in a tiny, one-bedroom apartment with twelve cats, is not the outcome I'm looking for. I'm not saying you should never date anyone in your younger years, never spend time with the opposite sex, or only court someone with the intention of marrying him or her. This misses the point entirely. There is no need to spend every Saturday night at home by yourself, sitting in the glow of scented candles, curled up in a blanket, reading your Bible, and spending hours in prayer. You needn't be a monk or a hermit or completely cut yourself off from the rest of the world to master the discipline of being single. What I'm saying is this. You must learn to be *secure in singleness*.

I want you to have good, successful relationships. I want you to date, have fun, be respectful, and build long-lasting friendships. But above all else, I want you to be comfortable with the idea of being single. The first step to becoming a confident, independent person is to reject the idea that you always need to be in a relationship. For some, this pressure is immense. Maybe it feels like all your friends are paired up with some guy or girl and the only way to fit in is to be in a relationship too. Perhaps it feels like your friends are busy every weekend because they're out having an awkward dinner at TGI Friday's with their boyfriends or girlfriends or staring longingly at each other over an overpriced latte. Perhaps when you talk to your friends at school, they tell you stuff like, "You'll understand once you start dating." Ouch, that's rough.

I understand that this may be difficult. I know it may seem like the pressure to pair up is insurmountable. But this is not a contest. There is nothing wrong with not being in a relationship or even not wanting to be in one, if that's the case. It doesn't mean there is anything wrong with you physically, socially, or emotionally. It is completely fine. You should not have to be in a relationship to win the approval of your friends. Most importantly, you don't have to have a boyfriend or girlfriend to be happy. This is a lie, and if you are going to be secure in your singleness, you must reject it as such. Your contentment and your fulfillment are not found in another person.

Here's the thing though. If you are to learn to be secure in singleness, you must first be single. You need to experience life without the emotional dependence a relationship carries with it. Being single for long stretches of time will help you learn to be independent. It gives you the chance to figure out who you truly want to be rather than who you want to be *for someone else*. It gives you the chance to be confident in who you are and the freedom to make choices on your own. If you spend your life being emotionally dependent on others, you will deprive yourself of the satisfaction of being independent. Just like a child who is given everything she wants is deprived of the gratification that comes with having worked, earned, and saved for what is hers, so too will you miss out on the gratification of emotional independence if you're constantly worried about finding the right person. When you forego the discipline of singleness, you forego the experience of being joyously unattached. You miss out on the fruit your newfound independence bears.

Independence builds the quality of character that only comes from knowing the full extent of your capabilities: from changing a tire or getting a job to paying your own way and providing for yourself. Sure, you may not want to spend the rest of your life on your own, but allow singleness to be your teacher for a while. Learn to be independent before you learn to be interdependent, lest you run the risk of being forever dependent on someone else for your emotional well-being. Interdependence is the result of two confident, independent individuals coming together, actively choosing to allow the other to meet their needs. It is a relationship of equals.

Emotional dependence, on the other hand, is an addict who is unable to garner the strength to overcome his addiction. He has a deep, uncontrollable, emotional need for his drug of choice with no corresponding physical need. That drug is the scraps of love thrown to him by a partner who does not necessarily share his addiction. It results in an unequal, passive, out-of-balance, and unhealthy relationship.

So if you are single, either by choice or circumstance, pour your energy into establishing emotional independence rather than using it solely to find your next date. It's time to break up with loneliness. It's time to kick dependence to the curb. It's time to reject the idea that it takes someone else to make you happy. It's time to be secure in your singleness and comfortable with yourself.

Get Serious, Just Not in High School

My younger brother ended up marrying his high school sweetheart. He was a football player, and she was a cheerleader. Classic. They maintained their relationship when he went off to Crazy-Go-Nuts University and she stayed behind to finish out her senior year in high school. When it came time for her to pick a school, she decided to follow him to Crazy-Go-Nuts U, where their relationship metamorphosed from budding young love to full-blown *Jerry Maguire* you-complete-me love. After graduation, they got married and literally rode off into the sunset on horseback. They are still happily married with three young children, living out their utopian existence in a house he built himself on a piece of land that stretches so far that nary a neighbor can be seen.

Why do I point this out? Because this is the exception rather than the rule. If you just came home from your first date with the boy or girl of your dreams, who is so perfect that you get the tingly-winglies just thinking about him or her, don't start naming your future children just yet. For the vast majority of people, it doesn't work out this way, despite how you may feel. That first love in high school makes you feel like you'll never stop feeling that way toward the object of your love. But feelings change.

No one can stop you from feeling this way. And reasoning with a person in this state is like reasoning with my anxiety-ridden, good-for-nothing stepdog. I'm more likely to receive a bite than a thank-you. All that I ask is this: don't let things get too serious between you and your significant other while you are still in high school. I don't care how great a guy he is. I don't care how sweet and athletic she is. There will be time for seriousness later.

You probably won't be the exception, like my brother and his wife. If you allow things to get too serious in high school, not only are you setting yourself up for heartbreak later, you'll add to the baggage you'll bring into your next relationship. Nobody wants to be the guy or girl *after* your five-year relationship with your high school sweetheart ends. That's a tough pill to swallow. It means you already gave your heart to someone else once, fully and completely. It'll leave him thinking, *Am I the runner-up? Is she settling for second place? Is she just in love with being in love? Or is she actually in love with me? Does she have any firsts left over to experience with me?*

Yes, you can get through all of that. The right guy or girl will overlook any past transgressions. But you can easily save yourselves the heartache and frustration of pouring yourself into a relationship that has the same odds of going the distance as you have racking up a million Twitter followers.

Though I joke about my brother and his wife living out a utopian existence, they would be the first to tell you that their life, like everyone else's, is not perfect. In fact, they are far, far different from the couple they started out as in high school. And that's a good thing. So before you go letting loose your anxious heart, let's agree to keep it casual, guard your heart (more on that later), and save the seriousness for after graduation.

Be Single in College

You don't have to be single the whole time, of course. I'm not a monster. However (and don't hate me when I say this), I do feel strongly that one of the best things you can do for yourself and your future spouse is to go off to college (or off to the real world, if college is not in your future) with no strings attached.

I can tell by your horrible gasps that you are actively resisting the urge to hurl this book into the fireplace. I get that this will be a very unpopular idea. Hard things aren't popular. If you are already single, great. Stay that way. But if your Facebook status says "in a relationship" as you're walking across that stage to collect your hard-earned high school diploma, consider pulling the plug on that before the summer's end.

Yikes! Did he really say that? That's awful!

No, it's not that awful. As we've discussed, the odds are not in your favor. At the Naval Academy, we had this thing called the 2 Percent Club. It was more of an idea than an actual club. The idea went something like this: of those people who start at the Naval

Academy with their high school sweethearts still attached, only 2 percent will still be in a relationship with their sweethearts in four years. 2 percent! I'm not sure anyone has done an analysis on this to determine what the actual number is, but I bet it's not far off. It would follow that everyone who goes off to college still committed to his or her high school boyfriend or girlfriend is striving to be in the 2 Percent Club. I'm not terribly good with numbers, but I think that means that roughly 98 percent of those who head off to school with a sweetheart in tow have a backpack full of disappointment waiting for them.

But that's not the only reason to cut the ties as you say your goodbyes. Again, I feel the need to explain what I'm not saying first so I'm not misunderstood. I'm not saying, "Don't bring sand to the beach." And by that, I mean I'm not telling you to go to college single because there will be hundreds of hot coeds there to welcome you. Don't break up with your boyfriend or girlfriend because you think you'll be able to easily upgrade to a better model. That's just mean. Though, if that is indeed your thought process, you should break up with your current fling because that's clearly all there is to you anyway. And if you're on the other side of that coin, I'd encourage you to ditch that loser. You are better off without him. Better yet, don't get involved with a person like that to begin with.

So we've established that the reason for you to begin quasi-adulthood single is not to see who else is out there. It's to be single! It's to go out into the world and learn who you are independently. People say you change during those first four years after leaving the safety and security of high school. I don't completely buy that. I think you simply become more of yourself. But to maximize the outcome of this metamorphosis, you need to cut the ties with your high school sweetheart.

You don't need to be mean about it. It could be as simple as saying something like this, "Well, I'm headed here after school, and you're headed there. Maybe we will still see each other occasionally, and we can talk to each other now and then, but I think I need to be single when I head off to school. I like you, and I don't want to do this so I can go date other people. I just need to be able to learn, grow, and figure out life on my own as an independent, capable person."

Whatever you do, don't say, "I need to go find myself." Not only is that a cop-out, it implies that you are lost. It brings up images of raging on PCP or stumbling back to your dorm room blackout drunk after a frat party. That is also not what I'm saying you should do. You should absolutely not do this, in fact. That is not finding yourself. That is finding a toilet to throw up in because you've been so irresponsible. That is abdicating all responsibility toward yourself. It's reckless and dangerous. Do not go find yourself.

Rather you already know who you are. This is your chance to grow further, to discover and nurture your strengths, and to dive into new interests in a setting that is away from your parents and old flames. It's a time to do your own laundry, wash your own sheets (and not just when you go home on holidays), prepare your own food, and pay your own way.

Oh, calling your old boyfriend or girlfriend every night before you go to sleep is not being single. You might think, *But it's okay. We aren't "dating" anymore. We're just friends!* Nope. Breaking up and cutting ties does not leave room for talking on the phone every night. Is he or she going to be sitting up, waiting for your call or text? Then you aren't broken up. You are still emotionally attached. It's simple, not easy. Break up fully and completely. I mean, if you still believe in fairy-tale Jesus and know that he's absolutely *the one* for you, then it shouldn't matter if you break up with him or not, right? Love, destiny, or fairy-tale Jesus will bring you back together again someday anyway. Sigh.

And even still, you have everything to gain by being away from him or her and being single for a while because, when fairy-tale Jesus does finally bring your struggling, lonely hearts back together again and you have a huge fairy-tale wedding, you'll both be a little more independent, a little more confident and ready to be interdependent with one another 'til death do you part.

I'm not stupid. I know that many of you will choose to completely ignore my advice on this. Because, after all, you're in love, and of course it will last forever. And following this advice and being single is hard! That's okay. Maybe for about 2 percent of you it will last forever, and you'll build a little house on a farm with your bare hands and raise organic, free-range chickens. And you'll have real dogs that don't bite you whenever you climb into bed. I won't argue with you.

But if you find yourself among the other 98 percent who go off to college and after many long-distance phone calls and texts, when you finally see each other again over Thanksgiving and observe that things are great at first but then just a little bit strange, and after you find yourselves sitting down over Christmas break, telling each other it's time to move on, then won't you please consider being single for just a little while? Don't go rushing back to your spring semester to talk to that girl in your chemistry class or that guy who always walks by your dorm on Tuesday and Thursday mornings at exactly 10:00 a.m. Just be single for a little while! Make some friends and hang out with them on weekends. Try some things you've always wanted to try but haven't gotten the chance. Join a club. Find a church. Study and have fun doing what *you* want to do. Most importantly, be comfortable. Be secure in your singleness. And yes, at some point, when you have mastered the discipline of being single, you're strengthened by confidence and sharpened by self-sufficiency, and you can honestly tell yourself you are happy just the way you are that you don't need someone else to make you happy, then you are ready for a relationship.

CHAPTER 8
Guard Your Heart

Above all else, guard your heart, for everything
you do flows from it.

—Proverbs 4:23

My sorry excuse for a stepdog tips the scales at ten pounds. Charlie's
poor little brain is probably about the size of a thimble, bless his
tiny little heart. Other than being bipolar and anxiety-ridden, his
hobbies include barking. Just barking. Science cannot yet explain
how it's possible for such a small mammal to have such a loud,
screeching, ear-piercing bark. He barks indiscriminately. He barks
at a knock at the door. He barks at anything that resembles a
knock at the door or the ring of a doorbell. (Watching *Wheel of
Fortune* is a disaster.) He barks at adults, children, birds, and other
dogs. You name it, Charlie barks at it. Sometimes when I let him
out in the backyard, he takes off at full speed, unleashed and
untethered, barking his head off. He'll run around randomly from
one end of the yard to the other, wildly and frantically barking at
the wind. It's pitiful.

Dogs like this shouldn't exist. It's science. Someone decided to
breed the tiniest, cutest little ball of fur possible, and in doing so,
this person bred out of him reason, intelligence, and any shred of
instinct his canine ancestors once possessed. Nature did not select
my stepdog. Some crazy, blue-haired French lady did. And now,

because of this undoing of nature, if I let him off his leash and set him free out into the wild, he wouldn't last a second. A coyote, a snake, a raccoon, or some large bird of prey would gobble him up, and there would be no more Charlie. Just a pile of curly, black, hypoallergenic fur. Pitiful.

My point is that Charlie needs me. He needs me to keep that leash on him so I can reign him in when he gets it in his thumbnail-sized medulla oblongata that he's going to bark at that German shepherd down the street; to tell him when to shut up and stop barking at the harmless Cub Scout at our door; and to hold him back when something shiny distracts him and he takes off across a busy street. If I let him go, he'd be toast. At best, he'd just run around barking at the wind.

When you've gained the fullness of confidence attained through the discipline of singleness, you will probably have come to notice an interesting phenomenon during your time spent avoiding relationships. Your heart is really dumb. In fact, your heart is a total idiot sometimes. You might say that your heart bears a strong resemblance to a ten-pound poodle. It is often crazy. It wants to make bad decisions. It doesn't always know what it wants or why it wants it. It's a loose cannon, and if you don't reign it back in, you will forever find yourself chasing after the wind. Like my dog, you have to keep your heart on its lead to protect it from itself. You have to talk some sense into it or allow others to speak to it because following it blindly across that busy street will lead to certain disaster.

You might have heard the phrase, "Follow your heart." You might have even heard it in a Disney movie. There may never have been three words more foolish and damaging as these. If you let your heart take the lead, if you chase after whatever feels good at the time, you will end up chasing after every whim and fancy, every little shiny thing that crosses your path. Follow your heart? It's not always the best advice. Lead it. Protect it. Guard it.

Falling in Love Doesn't Just Happen

What does it mean to guard your heart? It's a phrase that's probably overused and not well understood. It's certainly not easy. After all, we live in a follow-your-heart culture that tells us to toss good judgment aside and pursue whatever tugs at our hearts the most at any given point in time. We live in a culture where falling in love is expected, unavoidable, idolized, and idealized. But falling in love doesn't just happen. In fact, it is completely avoidable. Under the auspices of falling in love, we'll see what it truly means to guard your heart.

To help illustrate this point, consider fictitious Tom for a moment. Tom, a handsome young man, is filled with the energy and curiosity of youth. He is just about to finish the first semester of his junior year in college. On a beautiful Wednesday afternoon, Tom takes a break from preparing for his upcoming final exams and finds himself sipping a cup of coffee in the local college coffee shop. He glances up from his table and sees the most beautiful girl sitting a few tables over. Slender and stunning, she is gorgeous with green eyes and wavy, dark hair. At that same moment, she happens to look up and catches his glance.

Tom quickly realizes he has been staring and looks away. But he's pretty easy on the eyes, too, so the girl looks back, and their eyes meet once again. They both crack the slightest, slightly embarrassed little smile. After a few minutes of playing tag with their eyes, Tom finds the courage to get up and go talk to the girl. Her name is Amanda, and as they begin to chat, she says she was wondering if he'd ever come talk to her. This, of course, gives Tom the courage to ask if she has any plans on Friday night. Amanda, of course, does not, and their date is set.

After a night or two of unbearable impatience, Tom and Amanda finally go out on their first date. It's a bit slow at first, but then they get to talking, and before you know it, they are sitting on a bench outside her dorm. It's 2:00 a.m., and they've been talking and laughing for hours, though it only seems like a few minutes have passed. He understands her; she understands him. It's as if they've known each other their whole lives. They have fallen in love, fast and hard. It just happened.

Fast-forward a year or two, and they get married at a huge wedding that her parents so graciously paid for. Everything is perfect. Fast-forward a few more years, and their first baby arrives. Amanda states that she wants to stay at home, and Tom says he thinks they can make it work. And their lives are changed forever.

A few more years go by, and now the kids are five and two years old and starting to be quite a handful. Tom heads off to work early one morning and stops at the coffee shop to read the paper and escape the stress and chaos that is now his daily routine. He glances up from his paper, and sitting just a few tables over is the most beautiful young woman, just a few years younger than his wife. As he looks up, Tom finds her eyes staring right back at his. She smiles and looks down, but only for a second before she looks right back up. Tom's lips crack a polite smile. He sees her get up, walk toward him, and sit down in the empty chair next to him.

She says something like, "Haven't I seen you before at the gym?"

And he replies, "Oh, maybe so. I work out quite a bit."

And she says something like, "Yeah, I noticed."

They sit and talk for so long that Tom is late for work. The next day, same time, same place, there she is. He gets his coffee, and this time, he walks right over and sits down next to her as if she's expecting him. And she is.

Tom didn't know she would be there again this morning, but he had a suspicion. They talk and laugh, and all the problems and stress in Tom's life seem to fade into the distance for an hour. *It's okay*, he thinks, *because we're like friends. That's all. She understands me so well, and anyway it's only coffee.* Later it's only lunch and only on Fridays.

Fast-forward a little while, and Amanda begins to wonder

why Tom is so absent all the time, even when he's at home. Later at the divorce proceedings, after they have divvied up all their possessions and worked out the childcare schedule, she asks him, "Why?"

"I just fell in love," Tom replies. It just happened.

"What a bunch of bunk," you might be saying to yourself. And you'd be right because falling in love doesn't just happen. You let it happen. At some point, a choice is made to unleash the tethers of your heart and let that yapping poodle take off. Let's back up a bit and see how else this story could have played out.

Tom sees her get up, walk toward him, and sit down in the empty chair next to him.

She asks something like, "Haven't I seen you before at the gym?"

And he says, "Oh, maybe so. But if you'll excuse me, my wife just texted me, and I've got to give her a call. One of my kids just threw up on the dog!"

Tom gets up, grabs his phone, and heads for his car. The end.

Okay, maybe it doesn't have to happen exactly like this, but Tom knows when that little poodle inside his heart starts barking up the wrong tree. When that woman begins to walk over, in his mind he may be thinking, *Young. Check. Beautiful. Check. Attracted to me. Double check.* And that should be setting off alarm bells in Tom's mind, telling him he'd better get that leash out quick before something terrible happens. It's time to start guarding that heart.

Falling in love is no accident. I wholly admit that sometimes it can be incredibly difficult to control your emotions, and the emotions that flood your body when you are in love are some of the strongest of them all. Many great poets have captured what these emotions feel like, so I won't attempt to describe them in detail myself. But here's the deal. Just like anger, sadness, and depression, this too shall pass. Emotions come and go and rightfully so.

Being in love is no different. Those feelings are so strong at first that you think they will never go away, and yet they do.

The honeymoon phase always comes to an end. After all, if it didn't, who would ever get any work done? I don't mean that they are gone for good, but anyone who has been married for more than a second knows that you don't spend every hour of the day with hearts pitter-pattering for each other. Hopefully you can rekindle those emotions every now and then when the kids go to sleep early, but they are still just emotions. Wonderful, beautiful emotions.

So yes, falling in love, like any other emotion, can be difficult to avoid. But remember, it's the hard things that are worth doing. I'm not saying you should never allow yourself to fall in love. I'm saying you need to guard your heart and not let it get you into something that your head knows will be a total mess.

It's funny, the pushback I'll get when I say that falling in love doesn't just happen seems to evaporate when you throw marriage into the equation. It's as if you are expected to randomly fall for whoever comes along before you're married, but afterward, that switch is turned off. That switch doesn't just turn off. No, you don't get to choose who you will fall in love with. But guarding your heart is all about choosing who you *won't* allow yourself to fall in love with. That's not just possible. It's essential.

Whether you are married or single, the process of guarding your heart is the same. Guarding your heart means setting boundaries, learning to say no, avoiding the people you know are not good for you, and avoiding getting involved in any way with someone who is already married, abusive, or whose values are too different from your own, no matter how attractive he or she might be to you otherwise. Fairy-tale Jesus doesn't flip on a switch for the person He romantically sets aside just for you and switches it back off anytime your gaze falls on someone else.

As much as my wife wishes this were true, as much as she yearns that, when I saw other women, all I saw were big, black lines that covered everything but their eyes, feet, and any moles or terrible birthmarks they might have, sadly this isn't the case.

Thus, we are left with a choice: to fall prey to our gluttonous heart or to put up an active resistance. It's a choice you make every day.

You must choose to set up your own boundaries. Maybe that means you don't allow yourself to be alone with a certain person. Perhaps it means you need to choose a different lab partner. Maybe it means you only talk to that coworker when you're at work. Her text messages can wait until Monday.

These boundaries will look different for everyone. Only you know your limits. But here's the thing. If you know your limits, it's up to you to set boundaries that are way, way before your limits. No one builds a runway that's just barely long enough for a plane to land. Give yourself enough room so that, if you make a mistake, you don't go careening off the runway into the trees. If you set boundaries too close to your limits, one day you'll find yourself in a place you didn't expect, looking back at the hundreds of tiny decisions that baby-stepped your way long past the point at which you should have turned back. You'll look back at the simple choice you made to let your eyes linger for too long and later to let your mind linger for too long on that person you saw in the gym or at the airport.

Guarding your heart isn't easy. Holding a friend, acquaintance, or coworker at arm's length to make sure you don't let things go too far is hard. The counterparty may not fully understand why you don't open up to him or her. Do not worry. There are plenty of other people you can be best friends with. There's no need to be rude (most of the time), but holding someone at arm's length can be the wisest thing you'll ever do.

Be Cautious

Perhaps it was a good time in Tom and Amanda's lives to be looking for a serious relationship. But when you finally meet someone you're attracted to and your head and heart are finally in agreement, guarding your heart means you take it slow. Having learned to be secure in singleness should help keep you from diving heart-first into whatever relationship comes your way. That's what you used to do, back when you thought you needed someone else to make you happy. Now you have the discipline you need to go slow, to feel things out (emotionally!) and make sure it's right before making the decision—yes, the decision—to let your heart go a little further.

Guarding your heart gives you the freedom to be picky, and picky you should be. No one is perfect, so if you're holding out for someone who is six-foot-two with brown hair and blue eyes with an advanced degree who loves dogs, hates cats, enjoys sports but doesn't watch football, and wants to live three houses down from your parents, you might be waiting a while. Be picky, but also realistic. No one will check every single one of your boxes. Even if he or she does, you may one day find that one of the things you love most about your significant other also happens to be what annoys you the most about him or her. That laidback, carefree attitude you were so drawn to in college might eventually start to resemble laziness. That sense of humor is great when you're not trying to have a serious conversation. Instead of looking for someone to put a check in every one of your boxes, maybe you should consider whittling your list down to just the few things that are most important to you.

You can be picky without shutting yourself off to dating completely. I was very picky in college, but that doesn't mean I didn't go on any dates. (But seriously, my school was like 85 percent dudes. There weren't a lot of opportunities.) However, I could usually tell after one or two dates whether what was important to me was also important to her. If it weren't, then one or two dates was all she got. It's a lot easier to cut if off at that point than to let things build when they aren't quite right. If you're okay with being single, it makes it that much easier to pull the plug early instead of drowning slowly. No, that isn't mean or harsh. On the contrary, it's the best thing you could possibly do for both of you.

Loneliness

Maybe you have been single for far too long and you feel like a relationship is so far off that all this nonsense about being single and guarding your heart doesn't quite connect with you.

Don't despair. It's okay to feel lonely sometimes. It's *not* okay if it consumes you. It's *not* okay if, in the depths of worry and anxiety, you disregard the promises of God and seek acceptance elsewhere. Remember, God listens to our prayers. He knows the needs and desires of your heart before you even ask. And He is present in your loneliness.

There are two types of loneliness: burdensome loneliness, which must be overcome, and concurrent loneliness. Burdensome loneliness is the kind we've been talking about. It's the kind of loneliness that says you're not worthy unless some boy or girl out there loves you. It tells you your value is found in what others think of you. Burdensome loneliness compares your Saturday night at home by yourself to the couple's picture you see on Instagram. This is the kind of loneliness that has nothing of value to offer you and spreads lies that infiltrate your soul. Burdensome loneliness must be labeled as such, confronted and overcome. It is nothing but fear and anxiety disguised as a heart in need of rescue.

We've discussed at length how to overcome burdensome loneliness. We do it by seeking God and allowing Him to be our identity. We do it by allowing singleness to sharpen us until we are comfortable and secure in our own skin, lacking nothing. We overcome burdensome loneliness by guarding our hearts, setting boundaries, and not allowing just anyone in to temporarily fill that fear.

Concurrent loneliness, on the other hand, is merely a subtle reminder that there may be better things to come. Just before graduating college, one of my very best friends and I drove down to the Smoky Mountains for some hiking. We set out together, backpacks full, to get lost in the woods for a few days. When we reached our campsite on the first night, we set up camp by a beautiful river. We were the only people there that night in that backcountry campsite, and as the sun set, we lay on our backs on a big boulder, listening to the sound of the water gently flowing over the rocks and watching the sky turn dark. We stayed up late, watching shooting stars and satellites, talking about the deeper things in life, and listening to the quiet stillness of nature. Life is meant for nights like these, when the stillness of the night reflects the stillness in your heart, and all you feel is peace and gratitude.

In these moments, that concurrent loneliness can be felt. In the midst of feeling thankful to God for allowing you to spend this time with such a good friend, concurrent loneliness is the hopeful feeling in the back of your mind that one day you'll be able to spend a night like this with someone beautiful, whose hand you can hold while gazing up at the stars. Concurrent loneliness isn't overpowering. It takes a back seat to your present state of consciousness. There is no anxiety in it, only excitement. There is no fear, only the hope of what's to come. It's a patient yearning in the depths of your heart. Very simply, it's wanting a best friend that's pretty.

Concurrent loneliness is natural and good. There is nothing to be overcome here, as there is in burdensome loneliness. It simply tells you that perhaps you were designed to be one-half of a whole. If you're feeling this, it's okay.

If you are seeking God and earnestly asking Him to provide you a partner you can do life with, I believe He's listening. After all, "God sets the lonely in families" (Psalm 68:6). When you pray for discernment to see the needs of those around you, I believe He will place people in front of you with needs you can fill. Likewise, if you ask Him for a partner, a beautiful or handsome best friend, I believe He'll provide you those opportunities. No, the match won't be perfect by our standards. Life isn't a fairy tale. This might sound strange, but even some of the weirdest people I know have found someone equally as weird to spend the rest of their lives with.

But if you are feeling the impatient tug of burdensome loneliness on your heart, don't let your guard down for the first person who shows interest in you. "Desire without knowledge is not good—how much more will hasty feet miss the way!" (Proverbs 19:2). Burdensome loneliness leads to unguarded desire. Without the leash of knowledge around desire's neck, it's easy to make reckless and stupid decisions.

Being single can be difficult, and guarding your heart is no easy task. Falling in love is as easy as breathing under the right circumstances. But you have resolved yourself to be disciplined in doing hard things. The average person is content with inaction, complacency, and allowing life to happen to him or her. It's easy to sit in front of the television every night for two hours. It's easy to play video games instead of doing your homework. It's easy to eat whatever is convenient or whatever you're craving at the time. And yes, it's easy to throw yourself into relationship after relationship, looking for someone else to make you happy. The average person takes the easy way out. The average person is also overweight, underperforming to his or her potential, and unhappy. Don't be average. Be different. The easiest way to be successful in relationships, school, your family, and your job is not to take the easy way out. That's right. The easiest path to success isn't easy at all. It's hard!

But don't think that, once you've led your heart to the right person, decided to remove all the stops, and allowed yourself to fall in love, the rest will be all unicorns and rainbows. Like I said before, the honeymoon phase will end. And when it does, real life begins. And real life is messy. If you've done things right up to this point, then you're in good shape. But the beginning is still just the beginning, and relationships take hard work. A happy and successful relationship doesn't just happen. It is built one day at a time.

CHAPTER 9
Successful Relationships

Before we get too far, I should first pause here and define for you what I consider to be a successful relationship. After all, this could mean different things to different people. You may be thinking to yourself that a successful relationship is one that ends in marriage, but that's incomplete. That would mean that you only have one (hopefully) successful relationship in your whole life. Plus, if your marriage ends, you'd be hard-pressed to find someone who would call that a success. Then you might say a successful relationship is one that doesn't end at all. Yes, that would probably qualify as successful, but I believe the scope is broader than that. Let's get back to fictitious Tom for a moment.

Little did you know that, before fictitious Tom met Amanda, he had dated a few other women in the past. (I know, scandalous!) One girl, Kristen, was a bright young lady from a neighboring town whom Tom dated for almost a year. They met during their freshman orientation and connected quickly because, as it turns out, they had gone to rival high schools. Tom and Kristen spent much of their first few weeks of school together, learning to navigate the campus and their new lifestyle.

It was months and months later before they started dating, although Tom knew that Kristen was smitten with him almost from the start. He liked her too, but he did not want to pursue a relationship just yet since it was, after all, only the beginning of college and Tom wanted to be single for a while. He also wasn't sure that he liked her in any kind of romantic way.

As a gentleman, Tom tried not to lead on Kristen as best he could. He enjoyed her company, but he tried to leave it at that. As time went by, Kristen made it very clear that she wanted something more than friendship. They had been friends for quite a while.

It was nearing the end of their freshman year. Tom had been single the whole year and felt comfortable in his newfound independence, and he was happy with the relationships he'd built with new friends. He was open to dating someone but didn't feel like he'd met the right person yet. Still he had to admit that there was possibly something there between him and Kristen. *Maybe I just haven't allowed myself to open up to her yet,* he thought.

They had very similar interests and values. They aligned on the most important things, in fact. She was an attractive girl, Tom admitted, and many had confused them for a couple simply because they were often together. But Kristen's feelings for Tom were visibly stronger than his were for her. It was almost as if his feelings for her were more like that of a sister, to use the dreaded word.

But after some serious consideration, Tom thought he had to give it a shot. Perhaps he owed her the chance to see if there could be more to their relationship than just friendship. And so, Tom and Kristen finally began dating. It was fun and exciting. However, after six long months, Tom's feelings still hadn't changed. He knew Kristen had all but named their future children, and he wondered if she noticed that the gravity of their relationship was pulling at them unequally. He cared for her, for sure. He didn't want to hurt her and knew that breaking up would devastate her and possibly even ruin the friendship they'd developed. He wondered if he still hadn't given it the chance it deserved. He wondered— hoped even—if he might still wake up one day to discover that he loved her.

Tom kept it going for several more months. He kept it going even when Kristen would get discouraged with him, though she couldn't quite pinpoint why. It was as if he weren't quite there for her like she wanted him to be. She felt sometimes that he didn't treat her right or give her the care or attention that she required. It's not as if Tom didn't try. He just wasn't the type of guy to offer his comfort for her problems, most of which he thought were silly.

After nearly a year, Tom realized he had to call it quits. He liked her a lot. But he didn't love her. And he didn't want to continue a relationship where there was no chance of something better. So after days of agonizing over how to do it, Tom finally broke up with Kristen. And as he expected, she was devastated. It wasn't easy for Tom either. He knew it was the right decision, but he still cared for Kristen and didn't want to see her hurt. It's hard to spend a year closely tied to someone and not feel anything at all after deciding to part ways.

After the breakup, Tom gave Kristen some space. He didn't call her to make sure she was okay, though he thought about it. And neither of them jumped into a rebound relationship. He just let her move forward and tried to do so himself.

Was this a successful relationship? Yes! Was it perfect? What relationship is? A relationship doesn't have to be perfect to be successful. It was successful in that its beginning wasn't impulsive or foolish. Both Tom and Kristen's shared values made them compatible, and they were attracted to one another. (Yes, physical attraction is important.) Both Tom and Kristen seemed to earnestly like and respect each other, and Tom clearly tried to care for Kristen the way she needed to be cared for. In the end, Tom just wasn't right for her, and this is what made the end of the relationship successful. Successful relationships end when one or both people realize there isn't a future. Breaking someone's heart is never easy, but doing the right thing seldom is. In the end, it was what was required of Tom, like putting down a beloved pet when all that remains of its life is pain.

To sum up, successful relationships have a thoughtful beginning, unclouded by the visceral, erratic judgment of the heart. The heart has a say, of course, but the decision isn't his alone. Successful relationships are steeped in mutual respect, with two people who are ardently striving to meet one another's needs. They embody love in action. And when it's clear that there is no future, successful relationships end before they go too far.

To be clear, this relationship wasn't perfect. Tom would have done many things differently, but a successful relationship doesn't require perfection. Tom let things go on for too long and probably should have called it quits earlier. Maybe Kristen was trying too hard to force him to feel something for her that, deep down, she knew he didn't possess. The fact is that relationships don't fit neatly into a box. This relationship was successful in that these shortcomings did not define their relationship. They didn't ruin other relationships in their lives or fill their lives with baggage that will follow them like a third person into their next relationship.

Despite the pain that inevitably comes from a relationship that has ended, this particular flavor of pain serves to help us grow. Maybe that's the litmus test of a good relationship: does it produce pain that causes deep wounds that will leave a scar or pain that is here today and gone tomorrow and teaches us something valuable about ourselves?

If this were a successful relationship, what does an unsuccessful relationship look like? For Tom, it would have been to let his relationship with Kristen go on for another year, even though his heart wasn't in it. It would have been for him to hold onto it like a fish flapping in his hand, struggling to breathe and forcing it to work. Failure would have been to let their relationship go on for so long that, unfulfilled and frustrated, either Tom or Kristen decided to look outside their relationship for comfort before putting an end to their own first. Failure would have been to seek to patch the emotional holes with physical intimacy. Failure for them would have been to get married, which is maybe what Kristen desperately wanted, only to live out a marriage where affection is unequally doled out, where Tom is never quite able to meet her needs and expectations. Failure means settling for less than what God wants for you and ending up feeling trapped and alone.

Let's pause for a moment and look at another indication of what a failed relationship looks like. If a relationship is abusive—physically, emotionally, or verbally—it is a failure. There are few things in a committed relationship that should cause you to turn and run from it. Abuse is one of them. You should never settle for a boyfriend, a girlfriend, or a spouse who is abusive. You should never be afraid of the person who is supposed to love you and hold your best interest at heart. Fear has no place in a successful relationship. Do not stick around to try to change someone who is abusive. This person should figure that out on his or her own. And by leaving this person, not only do you protect yourself, you also send the message that what he or she is doing is unacceptable. Do not settle for the lie that you are responsible for someone else's behavior or you somehow deserve the abuse you're receiving. You are not responsible. It's not your fault. It's not your job nor is it in your power to change anyone. Don't stick it out. Don't wait. Leave.

While the confusion and pain associated with abusive relationships is far beyond the scope of this book, it's worth mentioning that it shouldn't be tolerated. I can't pretend to understand the complex psychology behind staying in an unhealthy relationship. All I can say is this. Do not think for a second that being miserable is normal or acceptable. When in doubt, pursue the objective opinion of a trusted friend or counselor. If your significant other is so controlling or abusive as to prevent you from seeking counsel, then you have your answer.

An unsuccessful relationship yields baggage. A successful one brings clarity. Both of which have a remarkable tendency to stick with you for a long, long time—the former like a pebble stuck in your shoe; the latter like a chance encounter with an old friend that comes just at the right time. This doesn't mean that there is never any pain associated with successful relationships. Pain is inevitable. Pain informs. Pain instructs. Pain directs. An unsuccessful relationship brings pain that isn't worth the cost. You wish it never happened. But a successful relationship is worth the pain that may come with eventually discovering it's not meant to be. The cost may be pain, but the reward is wisdom, and wisdom is more precious than silver. Yes, you can—and should—learn from both types of pain, but the latter can teach you all you need to know without leaving you with the regrets of the former.

In *The Problem of Pain*, C. S. Lewis writes, "God whispers to us in our pleasures, speaks in our conscience, but he shouts in our pain: it is His megaphone to rouse a deaf world."[1] What is God shouting to you through your pain? Maybe He's telling you it's time to start doing things His way instead of your own way. Maybe He's telling you that you've been searching for fulfillment in all the wrong places. Perhaps He's saying He wants something better for you. Maybe He's simply saying it's not the right time.

Dating can be fun and exciting, filled with the pleasure that comes with getting to know someone deeply, like uncovering a mystery. It can bring great joy and pain. But in any relationship, success is built, not stumbled upon. With intentionality, you can build successful relationships, and with intentionality, you can avoid unsuccessful ones.

---

[1] C. S. Lewis, *The Problem of Pain* (New York: HarperCollins, 1940), 91.

CHAPTER 10
Sex

It's time to get awkward. If you skipped ahead to this chapter because you just couldn't wait, that's okay. Just don't let that be a metaphor for your life. Some patience here is warranted, so let's not waste any time.

For starters, sex is great. In fact, sex is totally awesome. This needs to be said because I think that, in the best intentions of certain Christian circles, so much emphasis is placed on sexual immorality that we forget that God created sex for us. We, as parents, tend to panic at the thought of our children having sex before marriage and wrongly attempt to build up barriers for you in the form of fear and shame. Often in this area, we overwhelm you with truth and forego grace. But we desperately need to impart both, lest you grow up with so much guilt and shame for your natural desires that even a healthy sexual life within marriage eludes you.

So yes, sex is wonderful, fun, and exciting, and in the words of Solomon, "May your fountain be blessed, and may you rejoice in the wife of your youth. A loving doe, a graceful deer—may her breasts satisfy you always, may you ever be intoxicated with her love" (Proverbs 5:18–19).

Hey, it's in the Bible. And that's what we all want, right? To forever be intoxicated by the love of our lives. There is no better word to describe it than *intoxicated*. Not with drink or with drug, but with the love and beauty of the person who fully reciprocates your love. I want you to enjoy a beautiful, intoxicating, and healthy sex life, and yes, it should be enjoyed within the sanctity of marriage. This will be understandably difficult, given that the world has decisively chosen not to wait. Instead it has elevated sex to an idol, its not-so-subtle form of worship. But we are called to be different.

Culture today bombards us with sex, day and night. It doesn't matter where you are. Sex finds you—billboards; commercials; magazines; catalogs; daytime, prime time, or nighttime TV; books; movies; and of course the internet. Sex will find you wherever you are. There is no need to seek it out. It's literally everywhere. But if you do seek it out, there is no limit to what you might find.

In generations past, this was not the case. Sex used to be taboo. One could argue that that is the way it should be. It should be treated discretely or kept private. Others might argue that hiding it and never talking about it is just as unhealthy. Either way, I think it's fair to say that the pendulum has swung to the opposite side of the spectrum from where it once rested—far, far to the other side. The casualness with which sex is treated today is practically akin to breathing. Its pervasiveness is expected, and people may look at you like a fool at the mention of treating it with a little restraint. But the fact remains that sex is ubiquitous, and that's not likely to change anytime soon. As self-control is making its way toward the exits, replaced by impulsivity, we'd be wise to begin arming your generation with truth and knowledge surrounding sex rather than fear and shame. For fear is no match for truth. And when missteps occur, we are to meet them head-on with grace abundant.

Don't Eat the Marshmallow

Dr. Walter Mischel designed a famous psychological experiment dubbed "the marshmallow test" that was performed on preschoolers in the 1960s. A child was placed in an empty room with a researcher, and a single marshmallow or some other delicious treat was placed in front of him or her. The researcher explained that they were going to leave the room, and if the child could wait to eat the marshmallow sitting in front of him or her until the researcher returned about fifteen minutes later, then the child would get two marshmallows instead of one. By leaving the marshmallow sitting in front of the child while the researcher left the room, they presented a simple choice: succumb to the draws of instant gratification or exercise self-control.

The results were interesting. Those preschoolers who succeeded in delaying gratification went on to have higher SAT scores, along with a lower BMI, divorce rates, and addiction rates, than those who did not wait. Even more interesting, those children who could garner the self-control necessary to forgo their desires did so in very creative ways. Some children would push the marshmallow as far away from them as possible. Others would turn completely around in their chair so they couldn't see it. Still others would find ways to distract themselves from the temptation, for instance, by singing songs. But the implications of the experiment are far-reaching. It shows a link between one's ability to exercise self-control at an early age and their health and well-being later in life. And while some of us are probably wired to master self-control a little easier than others, it shows that certain strategies can be used and, in fact, learned by anyone with the intention of resisting temptation.

Waiting is hard. It's hard when you're a preschooler with a marshmallow sitting in front of you, and it's difficult when you're an adolescent and sexual temptation is all around you. But as Christians, we are called to wait. We are called to deny ourselves, time and time again, knowing that our physical bodies are just a temporary home to a spiritual being. We are called to wait to have sex for an undetermined amount of time until we are married. It's a call that has both spiritual and practical implications.

Popular culture has a far different perspective on sex, one that has taken hold of society's view on the subject. But one certainly can't expect people who don't share the faith to behave like Christians. (I just wish more Christians behaved like Christians.) But going forward, you will need to learn to recognize this cultural perspective for what it is and to replace it with God's perspective. And though pressures and temptations abound, you will need to adopt strategies to help you survive if you are going to resist eating the marshmallow.

Why Wait?

Spoiler alert: sex leads to babies. We know this to be true, and yet lust and pleasure seems to overshadow this most basic human function. Why? Because that's how sex is portrayed time and time again in the media. If you came to this planet from outer space, knowing nothing else about sex, what would you learn about it merely from watching TV? I think you'd conclude that sex exists solely for pleasure. While this notion isn't entirely wrong, as sex does provide pleasure, to think of sex merely in terms of visceral pleasure is a mistake. In fact, last time I checked, 100 percent of the seven billion people on the earth today are here because of sex, save the few who got a little help from science when nature wasn't enough.

God wants us to enjoy the things He created the way He intended them to be enjoyed. He gives us commands and directions to follow because He knows what's best for us and wants us to avoid the path that leads to unnecessary, self-inflicted pain. So how does He intend for us to enjoy it? What is sex for?

Intimacy

Spiritually, sex is the most intimate act one can share with another person. The more you love someone, the more intimate your relationship becomes. This intimacy, this intensely personal and private relationship shared with the person you love, makes sex so powerful. There is no more intimate act than when two become one. The act is reflective of the relationship it represents, baring oneself fully to another, flaws and all, and being accepted. And like all intimate things, its intimacy is cheapened when it's shared outside of that relationship; when it ceases to be personal. It's like when a close friend whispers a secret in your ear, only to find out later that you are the third or fourth person she's told. Was the secret really that special, personal, or intimate? Was it really a secret at all?

Throughout the New Testament, Christ is referred to as the bridegroom, waiting on us, His church, as His bride. It's interesting that God's chosen analogy for His relationship with us is that of a bridegroom and bride, not husband and wife. I don't think the relationship of a husband and wife is any less intimate than that of bride and groom. It's just normal. Routine. Maybe even a little complacent at times. But a bride and bridegroom? That's fresh and new. It conjures up images of weddings, celebrations, newness, youthful passion, resounding love, and, yes, the wedding night.

God compares His relationship with us to that of a bride and groom on their wedding night. It's as if He's saying, "Come to me, flaws and all. Bare yourself completely to me because I want every single part of you." Nothing is more intimate than that. And make no mistake, His desire is to have an intimate relationship with us. It's as if He designed sex specifically to be a spiritual connection through a physical act.

This intimacy provides the intense emotional connection between husband and wife. Sex is a way in which you can show your love, your commitment, your need, and your gratitude to your spouse. It's a gift to be treasured, guarded, and protected.

Procreation

Aside from the spiritual, which is really all you need, there is a practical side to waiting until marriage as well. If you were to give in to your every sexual desire, not only would you be lacking true intimacy with anyone, frankly, you'd run the risk of having children with multiple people. This sounds silly, but only with respect to the lens with which sex is viewed in our culture today, where sex is solely for pleasure.

But it's not just for pleasure. It's also for procreation. And it can be quite difficult to prevent the latter if your intent is only to enjoy the former. Sure, there are ways to prevent pregnancy and disease, but none of them is foolproof.

If you want to see what a complicated life looks like, have children with more than one person. Try to raise children together with multiple baby daddies or baby mommas. Shuttle your kids back and forth from Mom's house to Dad's house. Work out all those holiday schedules and parent-teacher conferences, and be sure to save some time for the fights and disagreements that will spring up along the way. Now that's hard. Certainly it's doable. People do it every day. But practically speaking, it's much easier for you to live with the father or mother of your children together in one place. Enough said.

Pleasure

This reason needs no introduction, as I've mentioned, because it gets all the attention from popular culture. It's hardly worth mentioning except to note that it isn't the only reason for sex. But yes, sex is also for pleasure. It can be an outlet to relieve the body of stress. And it can also be just plain old fun.

There are other reasons for sex: to guard against marital insecurity; to reunite after conflict; or to heal from emotional wounds. But regardless of the reason, as Christians, we are to wait until marriage. Of all the good and practical reasons to wait, foremost among them is this. We were not meant to submit to our body's every desire. Our bodies were meant to submit to us and us to God. "Those who live according to the flesh have their minds set on what the flesh desires; but those who live in accordance with the spirit have their minds set on what the spirit desires" (Romans 8:5).

Sex is not bad, evil, or ugly, but it is much more than a physical act. We weren't called to succumb to our every fleshly desire. We were called to be spiritual beings. Denying our bodies requires self-control, and the world has shunned self-control. But you were called to a greater purpose than to live in conformity with the world.

I could tell you how great and wonderful it is to wait and how perfect your reward will be when you finally fall in love and get married. However, while I generally believe this to be true, here again we start to run into fairy-tale Jesus, whose sole purpose, apparently, is to give us everything our hearts desire. The typical script for Christian sex is to bombard you with guilt and fear and then tell you that your reward for maintaining your virginity is that your wedding night will be perfect and you will live happily ever after.

I see two problems with this. First, life isn't always so rosy and perfect. In most cases, yes, I think your wedding night will be fantastic. But sometimes life doesn't get that memo. Life tends to disregard fairness. Second, fairy tales aside, we are called to control our bodies. Period. We are called to live according to the spirit, before and after we are married. It is not something we do to achieve a reward at the end.

Yes, I want your wedding night to be special and perfect and your marriage to be one filled with love and intimacy of the deepest kind. But more importantly, I want you to live according to God's good and perfect will, knowing that His plans are good and His path is straight. That should be all you need to know.

So You Messed Up

You ate the marshmallow, didn't you? Don't look at me with those powdery white lips and tell me you didn't. You messed up. Maybe you went too far. Perhaps you went all the way. Maybe it was with your boyfriend or girlfriend. Or Maybe it wasn't. Mistakes happen, and choices are made. Perhaps you're wrought with guilt, wondering how you, a good Christian person, could have allowed that night to happen. You feel like you're not good or worthy enough anymore for God, your friends, or your future spouse.

And you know what? You're right. You aren't good enough. In fact, none of us is good enough. Jesus (the real one, not the fairy-tale one) set the bar pretty high when he said, "Anyone who looks at a woman lustfully has already committed adultery with her in his heart" (Matthew 5:28). We all fall short of this standard. Even if you are squeaky clean on the outside, God sees the heart. So before you lament your own shortcomings, claim innocence, or point the finger at another, search your own heart first.

Thankfully, when we stumble, grace is there to pick us back up. Though the bar is set high, our God is a God of forgiveness. Despite what you did or wanted to do or how far you went, your sin is not so great as to separate you from your loving Father. Now that is a lesson some of our earthly fathers could use a little more of sometimes. No, we cannot deny the truth, but we can accept grace. We cannot always undo the earthly (practical) consequences of our actions, but our spirit can have peace knowing that His forgiveness covers us. When you have sincerely asked for and received forgiveness, there is no longer a reason to feel guilt or shame. You may still have to face the reality of the situation, but you can do so with a clean heart.

So you messed up. It won't be the last time you make a mistake, I assure you. But before we go any further, let me be clear on what this *doesn't* mean for your life.

It doesn't mean you are a terrible person. You had sex before marriage. You fooled around. Maybe you made some very bad decisions, but that does not make you a bad person. You are not the sum of your past failures. We tend to elevate sexual sins above all others. But sin is sin, and according to Jesus, even lust of the heart is adultery, and His grace covers that too. Do not be fooled into thinking that, because of your bad deeds, you can never be good or no one will love you if he or she finds out the truth. No, you are not a terrible person. You are just a person—a person who is about to meet the most powerful force in the world, forgiveness.

It doesn't mean you have to marry that person! You may be chuckling to yourself right now, but I'm dead serious. Perhaps you and your boyfriend or girlfriend went too far. It doesn't mean you must marry that person! You may be thinking to yourself, *Oh no! I had sex before marriage! How can I make this right? If we get married, then it will be okay, right? Then it won't have been a mistake. At least not a big one. He'll be the only guy I've ever slept with. I can make it right by marrying him.*

Wrong! If you think this sounds crazy, you're right! But someone is thinking this very thing right now. Do not let a mistake—and yes, it was a mistake—lead you into another mistake. There is no logic in that. If your relationship isn't right, it's not right. Do not hang on to a sputtering train wreck of a relationship simply because you lost your virginity to someone. That is a terrible reason to get married. In fact, sex is never a good reason to get married. Don't get married because you had it, and don't get married because you want it. Get married because you want to spend the rest of your life with someone.

Yes, it's always hard to admit to yourself that you messed up. It's hard to end a relationship after you've allowed yourself to get too comfortable physically. As we know, sex is intimate. Once you've experienced that level of intimacy with someone, it's hard to let that someone go, even if you know he or she is not the right person for you. But sex should never be your excuse for staying in a relationship that isn't right.

It doesn't mean you can't have a great marriage! You thought your last girlfriend was the one. You loved her and knew deep down that you were going to marry her. You'd been together for years, and it felt so right when the two of you decided to have sex. It didn't seem wrong at all. Not at the time. You never expected the relationship to end, and now that it has, you wonder if you have ruined any chance you had at having a truly intimate relationship with someone when you finally do get married. You dread the conversation you'll have to have with her and the look that will surely cover her face when you tell her that you're sorry but you didn't wait.

Yes, that will be a difficult conversation, one that would be easier not to have to have. But do not think for a second that you can never find true intimacy with another person just because you didn't wait. Your sexual past does not have to define your future marriage. Your marriage can still be great, wonderful, and new. And yes, sex can still be spectacular. You can experience intimacy like never before and find forgiveness and acceptance, flaws and all.

Do not underestimate the healing power of God. The true work of miracles is not how He magically brings two perfect people together to live happily ever after. No, we have already dispelled that myth. The true work of miracles is how He takes two imperfect people and changes their hearts. You won't find fairy-tale, matchmaker Jesus anywhere in the New Testament, but you will find heart after heart changed, healed, and made new.

Perhaps you're the person on the other side of the coin, who has waited diligently and dutifully, only to discover that the one you waited for did not wait for you. You need to know that sometimes grace extended is just as powerful as grace received. Forgiveness works both ways. When you make the decision to forgive someone else, your heart can be supernaturally changed every bit as much as theirs. Remember, intimacy is baring yourself to another, flaws and all, and being *accepted*. You both will have flaws. Some will be easier to accept than others are. But true intimacy can never be achieved without forgiveness. You can't hold on to grudges and past offenses, lording them over your spouse's head, and still expect to experience true intimacy.

My first dog, who not surprisingly was quite the opposite of my current dog, was an amazing creature. She was obedient, playful, smart as could be, and a dutiful and talented hunter. She was the perfect companion. However, on one occasion, she decided to poke her nose where it shouldn't have been and got herself popped in the nose by a mousetrap. She came running through the kitchen, whimpering, with that mousetrap clamped to the side of her poor little lip. Despite it being stuck to her lip, she had managed to get what she could of it in her jaws, and she was holding onto it for dear life, as if to say, "I got it! But it has me!" Little did she know, though it might have felt a little better for her to hold that which caused her pain tightly in her teeth, the first step toward healing was to let it go.

It feels good sometimes to hold onto those grudges, to harbor that anger or bitterness in your heart. Sometimes you just don't want to let it go. When you do, you release the self-righteous judgment you'd so dearly staked your claim to. But if that grudge is toward the person you've committed the rest of your life to, it will spill over into every aspect of your marriage. You must let go of the mousetrap and let the healing take its course. Forgiveness is powerful. Whether you must forgive yourself or someone else, there is a supernatural power in it that surpasses understanding.

Of course, it's always better not to have to forgive or ask for forgiveness in the first place. Life is easier when you get things right the first time. Though waiting is hard, it is possible, despite what others may tell you. Let everyone else take the easy road. You take the hard one. But if you stumble, remember that grace covers a multitude of sins. You can still have the marriage you always wanted without the guilt or stains of your past.

Waiting until Marriage: How to Avoid the Hanky Panky

Nobody said life was going to be easy when you started following God. (Someone might have said that, but they were wrong). Living the #ChristianLife doesn't mean you'll be adding #Blessed to all your Facebook posts. Also please don't do that. It's really annoying.

Frankly, living the Christian life can be downright hard, as we're expected to do things like turn the other cheek, love our enemies, forgive those who curse us, welcome persecution, and give at least 10 percent of our income away. That stuff's hard! But when you are smack dab in the middle of that hormone-fueled phase of life with temptations all around you, it can feel like the most difficult thing in the world is simply waiting to have sex until marriage.

The first thing you need to know is that it is certainly possible. Many people have done it. Sometimes all it takes is someone to prove to you that you can do it.

In the early fifties, no one at that point had ever run a sub-four-minute mile. In fact, no one even knew if it were even humanly possible to do so. But on May 6, 1954, Roger Bannister became the first person ever to break four minutes, running the mile in 3 minutes and 59.4 seconds. How long was it before someone else came along and did it? About a month. On June 21 of the same year, John Landy became the second man ever to break the four-minute threshold. Since then, it has been broken again and again, with the current world record sitting nearly seventeen seconds under the four-minute mark.

A funny thing happens in the human mind once it realizes that something is truly possible. It's as if those mental barriers are removed, allowing your body to reach its full potential. Getting past that mental hurdle is the hardest part because, if you believe something to be impossible, for you, it most definitely will be. Bannister didn't just wake up one morning and run a sub-four-minute mile. He knew he could break it. He knew it was possible to push his body just a little bit harder than he had before, to endure that pain just a little bit longer. Of course, once he did it, many others realized the same thing and followed suit. All it took was one person to shatter that mental barrier for everyone.

Your average person cannot run a four-minute mile. Luckily, waiting to have sex until marriage is not nearly the test of physical endurance that running is. Though if you were to take your cues from our culture, you may be led to believe that such a feat is nearly impossible or at the very least improbable. Just think how many movies there are where the sole plotline rests on one character setting out to lose his virginity. Our culture actively encourages us not to wait. With all that pressure, it's easy to forget that waiting is possible.

You can do many things to avoid the temptations around you. The first is to find someone out there who will help keep you accountable. Find a good friend who will support and encourage you. Life is hard enough as it is, but without anyone encouraging you to do the right thing, it's almost impossible to make it out alive. This person should share your beliefs and be accessible to you. This should be a person you trust and feel comfortable confiding in. It might be a group of people who get together regularly to commiserate each other's struggles and celebrate one another's victories. Finding accountability is paramount to your success on many levels, especially remaining steadfast in your commitment to wait.

Be sure to communicate your convictions with the person you are dating. This person should know that you are committed to saving yourself until marriage, and hopefully the people you choose to date will also share your values, right? So if the one you're dating is also pressuring you to have sex, that is a red flag. Even if this person doesn't share your beliefs, which he or she should, your boyfriend or girlfriend should at least respect you enough to want you to keep your commitments. It's hard enough resisting the pressure of friends and culture urging you to do it. You don't need that pressure from your boyfriend or girlfriend.

Set boundaries with that person. When you're living under your parents' roof, that means following their boundaries for you. But when you're off living on your own, you would be wise to set your own boundaries. Only you know the extent of your self-control. Maybe you should avoid being alone in your dorm room or apartment with your significant other. Perhaps you shouldn't allow that goodnight kiss to go on for thirty minutes. I don't know, but you do. Give it some thought, discuss it with your boyfriend or girlfriend, and figure out where you need to draw that line. I won't do it for you. But be completely honest with yourself.

Here's the deal: if you find that you keep rocketing past your safe zone and dipping your toes in the deep end of the pool, perhaps you need to be a little more aggressive with those boundaries and move them back a step or two (or three). And once you set them, adhere to them!

One helpful way to delay the hibbidy dibbidy is to avoid watching bad movies. Remember those preschoolers who could withstand the marshmallow test? They would push that marshmallow as far away from themselves as possible. They would turn around in their chairs so they wouldn't have to see it. Watching that flesh-filled movie, the kind disguised as a summer blockbuster, is like placing that marshmallow on a beautiful platter, setting it right in front of you, and letting yourself salivate over it. There's no better way to set those hormones on fire than to curl up with that hot babe next to you on the couch with her sweet-smelling hair on your shoulder while watching that fleshy sex scene in your favorite HBO series. Oh, and make sure it's late at night in your dorm room while your roommate is gone for the weekend. It's like drizzling that marshmallow with chocolate syrup and adding two scoops of vanilla ice cream next to it. It's a surefire way to test the limits of temptation.

Step away from the marshmallow! Are you *trying* to eat that marshmallow? Or are you trying to get so close to it that you can just imagine what it tastes like? Apparently preschoolers are a lot smarter than we give them credit for. I'm telling you, if you set that marshmallow on the edge of your bed every night, you will eventually eat it. No one has that kind of self-control.

And yet, like many other things, watching and talking about such shows and movies has become commonplace, even among

Christians. Waiting is hard enough as it is. Don't make it harder by filling your mind with those images.

Also, no sexting, for all the reasons I've already cited and more. The last thing you need is someone sending you high-definition pictures of the very marshmallow you are trying to distance yourself from. Plus, you never know where those images will go after you hit send or after your boyfriend becomes your ex-boyfriend. No late-night "What are you wearing ;-)" texts either. You can only dip your toes in the water for so long before it starts to get boring, becomes normal or comfortable, or feels no longer enough. Next thing you know, you'll find yourself wading into the deep end together in your skivvy shorts. It starts to get chilly, and the only way to get warmer is to take those off too! You get the picture. Sexting leads to babies.

Finally, for crying out loud, just keep your clothes on. It seems pretty simple, but the best way to forego the horizontal tango is to keep your clothes on—buttons buttoned and zippers zipped. Lord, have mercy! It's hot in here. I think it's about time we jump to another subject. I can only blush for so long.

CHAPTER 11
Pornography

Well, I told you things were gonna get awkward. This subject has become one we can no longer avoid. If you're reading this, odds are, you've viewed it already. Boy? Girl? It doesn't matter. It's not just a problem for guys. Why have you already seen it? Because the internet is flooded with it. It might take you a few minutes of Googling to find some good information for that research project you're writing, but it will only take you about 0.2 seconds to find thousands of sites that would make your grandmother's eyeballs hit the floor. You've seen porn because it's easy. Maybe you didn't even look for it. It just found you. If you're a parent of a teenager, I hate to break it to you, but chances are good that your son or daughter has already looked at porn.

The story used to go something like this. I was hanging out at my friend's house when we stumbled upon some magazines his older brother had stashed in the back of his closet. Now it probably sounds a little more like this. I was sitting in the locker room when my friend turned around and showed me a picture he had on his phone that made my jaw drop. Bye-bye, innocence.

I could give you all the statistics, like how the average age of first exposure to porn for boys is twelve.[2] Or how 93 percent of

---

[2] Elizabeth M. Morgan, "Association between young adults' use of sexually explicit materials and their sexual preferences, behaviors, and satisfaction," *Journal of Sex Research* 48 (2011): 520–530.

boys and 62 percent of girls will be exposed to porn before they turn eighteen.[3] I could tell you about all the studies that have been done that show porn's effects on the adolescent brain, how it can become a very real, chemical-like addiction. These things are all good to know. But the reality is, when you saw that first pornographic image when you were too young to fully grasp it, you were flooded with all kinds of thoughts and feelings. Foremost among them was the inherent understanding that what you were doing was wrong.

I'm going to make a jump here, without evidence or argument, and tell you that pornography is bad for you. It's bad for you at any age, but it is especially damaging to kids, who are either way too young to understand what they're seeing or old enough to have their preconceived notions of what sex is and what it should be completely derailed by pure sexual fantasy. It's harmful, and it's a problem that, I daresay, everyone of your generation will have to face in one way or another.

There's no need to define for you what porn is and isn't. To borrow from former Supreme Court Justice Potter Stewart, you know it when you see it. I would add that, just because an image may not necessarily be considered porn by our culture's loose standards (for instance, that billboard or advertisement you see every day), that doesn't mean it can't stir up that same sexual excitement.

Images inundate us. Every time you turn around, a celebrity or just an ordinary person for that matter has posted a racy photo of himself or herself on Instagram, which somehow makes it onto your news feed. It's unavoidable and harder than ever for a teenager these days, let alone an adult, to filter out such things. It's as if every day there is a battle raging for your mind and eyes. But it is a battle that must be fought within each of us.

---

[3] Chiara Sabina, Janis Wolak, and David Finkelhor, "The nature and dynamics of Internet pornography exposure for youth," *CyberPsychology and Behavior* 11 (2008): 691–693.

One of the most harmful things about porn is its incredible ability to completely objectify women. Boys are the biggest consumers of porn, and thus girls are overwhelmingly its stars (or victims). These girls aren't there because of their intelligence. They don't appear in these videos for their talents or ideas. They are in them for their bodies, plain and simple. They are cast for their ability to stir up sexual desire in men. But they don't get much of a say in how their bodies are treated on film.

When I say that women are objectified in porn, I mean it in a very literal sense. Their bodies are treated in the most debasing, inanimate way possible, solely to serve the elaborate, unrealistic, and demeaning sexual fantasies of the men they are selling themselves to. These women are treated purely as sexual objects, like toys to feed someone else's desires.

What does it do to a boy's mind to witness this type of objectification over and over again? What does it do to a girl's mind? Might she think that her role in this world is purely a sexual one? Can it serve any good purpose, or does it contribute to a catcalling culture of disrespect? If you told your son again and again that a woman's value lies in her physical appearance, he would likely come to believe it. If you told him repeatedly that women exist to serve him and their ideas and aspirations have no merit, he may one day believe it. This is the message of pornography. It's a message that kids are receiving at a very young age whenever they consume it. If they become addicted, it's the message they'll receive over and over, so much so that they may one day believe it.

Another danger that exists is that porn's portrayal of sex creates an unrealistic expectation in a young person's mind of what a true, intimate physical relationship looks like. To put it bluntly, sex depicted in porn isn't real. Though viewing it may stir up excitement and temporarily feed your lust and desire for sexual gratification, in all likelihood, what you are viewing is completely unrealistic and probably even very painful. In fact, often men who become addicted to porn crave it so badly that it becomes the only way for them to find any sexual satisfaction at all. It has damaged their minds so completely that not even the real thing can satisfy them anymore. Only the fantasy.

So if you are a young man or woman who is viewing porn on a regular basis, you must know that it is in no way an accurate depiction of the healthy, satisfying sexual relationship you might expect in marriage. To continue to feed your lust in that way will only serve to destroy intimacy.

If you are a regular consumer of porn, don't think that it's not a problem or it's something you can just stop once you get married and your spouse suddenly fulfills your desires. That's a losing argument. First, you may not even know the damage it's causing you right now. Second, it's naïve to think that you will simply stop once you've been in the habit for so long. Maybe you're not even in a relationship, though you hope to be in one someday and you think you'll stop when that day comes. Ask yourself, "Is what I'm doing today honoring my future girlfriend? Is it respectful to her?"

Sure, you may not even know her yet, but what if you met her tomorrow? Would you be ashamed about what you looked at today? If you are trying to be *the one* or pursue *the one*, then pornography should have no part in your life.

If you have tried and tried to stop but just can't seem to shake it, it's time to take drastic measures. "If your right eye causes you to stumble, gouge it out and throw it away. It is better for you to lose one part of your body than for your whole body to be thrown into hell" (Matthew 5:29). No, I'm not suggesting that you should cut out your eyes. This verse tells us that we should exhaust every measure to rid ourselves of sin, and this is the perfect example. It's time to get accountability. Does your phone cause you to sin? Get rid of it. Downgrade to a "dumb phone." Is Facebook a trigger for you? Delete it. Get some software installed on your computer that sends the sites you visit to a friend. Do certain TV shows tend to stir up these desires? Get them out of your life. Tell your friends you won't watch with them anymore. Get extreme. Declare war on porn, and win the battle for your mind.

There is another side of porn that you may not even be aware of. It is the dark side of a dark industry. Human trafficking is a problem that is likely as old as humans, and it is still very much alive today. What is it? It's modern-day slavery, and it is prevalent all over the world. Yes, even here in the United States. Women and girls are tricked, coerced, blackmailed, kidnapped, and controlled. They are forced into sex slavery and controlled with drugs, alcohol, threats, and abuse. The fact is, you don't always know whether the women you are watching are victims or willful participants. You are led to believe that these women are willfully engaging in consensual sexual acts. You are led to believe that they take pleasure from all the things they do and have done to them. But in truth, you may well be watching a woman or a girl who is being forced to do these things against her will. You may be watching a slave. Porn fuels the illegal, immoral, and dehumanizing sex trade industry that affects millions around the world. It's a fact and something you must be aware of.

Porn is bad for you. It is destructive to your mind, your family, your spouse, your girlfriend or boyfriend, or even to your very soul. It can steal your life away from you and offer absolutely nothing in return. Porn will never satisfy you. In fact, the more you consume it, the less it will satisfy you. And the less it satisfies you, the more you will crave it. When you are thirsty, a drink of water will quench your thirst, leaving you satisfied and no longer yearning for a drink. Porn offers you no such resolution. That short, fleeting, fickle hit to your brain is a powerful one, one that your brain will work hard to feel again.

Many things can grab hold of your life, take control away from you, and utterly consume you, but few that are so efficient at it as porn. Most of these things aren't bad in and of themselves. Money, for instance, is amoral. It's neither good nor bad. You can wisely store it up, use it to support your family, or give it to the needy. But if you let it, the love of it or the pursuit of it can lead you to ruin. Social media is another good example. It can be used to share love, goodness, truth, and awareness, or it can be used to spread hate, slander, and deception. It too can overpower and consume you if you let it. You can even allow your career to consume your life, leaving a stream of broken relationships in your wake. But none of these things is bad in and of itself. Each one has just as much capacity for good as it does for evil.

But with porn, there is no upside. It will promise you pleasure and deliver only destruction. It serves only to debase, objectify, enslave, and devalue, both those who consume it and those who create it. It will take your money, your dignity, your relationships, and your reputation if you let it. Porn is a one-way ticket to a destination that's always just a little further away. There is no good in it. Get it out of your life.

We humans are very good at justifying things to ourselves. We say to ourselves, "Yes, I deserve this piece of cake because I worked hard or had a bad day." We tell ourselves we need that nicer car or bigger house when what we really mean is, "I need that because I *want* it." We tell ourselves that watching this show or that movie is okay, despite those scenes that are scattered throughout. We'll say to ourselves that it's okay to visit that website because it's not really porn. It's art. It's beautiful, not pornographic.

God doesn't see things the way we do. We may pat ourselves on the back for spending thirty minutes staring at celebrities in their underwear because, hey, it could have been worse. We say it's okay to watch that show even though it's filled with sex because the story is really good, the actors are great, and the writing is second to none. You don't watch it for the sex scenes anyway.

But God says this, "But I tell you that anyone who looks at a woman lustfully has already committed adultery with her in his heart" (Matthew 5:28). That's a pretty high standard. Ask yourself, "Can I really watch this show without the slightest bit of sexual excitement or lust in my heart?" By watching someone else's daughter undress right on the screen in front of me, am I condoning and accepting as truth what our culture says is okay? This is a question I think I've answered for myself, and I will leave you to answer for yourself.

There is no doubt in my mind that porn is unhealthy. It's not necessary to repeat it. But I wonder, because it's so easy to find and consume and so extreme compared to generations past, has it completely transformed our culture without us even realizing it? I wonder if it hasn't completely reset the boundaries of decency and prudence, shifting the starting line of cultural relativism. After all, no matter how much skin is shown and how much is left to the imagination, we all know it could be worse. Relativism is how our justification starts. It's the "I may do *this*, but I don't do *that*" argument we set for ourselves in our mind. It's the *that* that porn has grabbed a hold of and dragged without much resistance, far, far to the left. And with it, our *this* has followed it obediently.

The greater the pleasure, the greater the pain. The more power something has for good, the greater its capacity is for evil. Nuclear physics brought us an almost unlimited source of power to provide good, clean energy to millions all over the world. But with that same power, that same science, comes the capacity to create weapons that could literally wipe humanity from the face of the earth. Make no mistake. Sex is a great and wonderful gift that God has given us. But such a wonderful gift, when used incorrectly, can cause a great deal of pain. It's these good things like sex that must be safely guarded, responsibly used, and treated with the respect they deserve.

I want you to enjoy a satisfying, fulfilling sex life within the bounds of a healthy marriage. I want you to view sex not as something to be consumed but something to be shared with the person closest to you. I want you to view sex not through the lens of cultural or moral relativism but through the unshakable truth and understanding of God's Word.

CHAPTER 12
Marriage

> By wisdom a house is built, and through understanding it is established; through knowledge its rooms are filled with rare and beautiful treasures.
>
> —Proverbs 24:21

Two things happened when I got married: I got a friend for life, and I was never on time for church again. My wife and I have been married for ten years, which means we've been late to church about five hundred times now. We met at a wedding. I was a groomsman, and she was a bridesmaid. Classic, I know. At the time, I was in flight school in Pensacola, Florida, having graduated from Annapolis a year and a half earlier, and she was a (hot) young nurse working in Birmingham. She had caught my eye the night before the wedding, the evening we met, at the rehearsal. She was related to the bride-to-be, so most of her family was also in attendance later at the rehearsal dinner. All the groomsmen sat at a table with the bridesmaids, and we tried our best to beat our chests while not making complete fools of ourselves. She caught my eye because she was gorgeous and I could tell that her family was important to her. I'd see her step away from the raucous occasionally to sit and chat with her grandparents.

The next day, following the wedding reception, there was a small party for all the groomsmen and bridesmaids. We talked, ate, and played games together, and by some miracle, when the party was over, I gathered up the courage to ask if I could give her a call sometime. And by some miracle, she said yes.

We spent the next few months driving back and forth from Pensacola to Birmingham to see each other. On one of our early dates, I took her to a quiet beach, away from the crowds. It was a beautiful day, and the water was warm, so I convinced her to head into the water with me. The sun was high, and I grabbed her hand as we waded out into the surf. I soon discovered that, the further we got from the beach, the closer she got to me.

Cool, I thought.

I kept going deeper, out into the big swells, and she grabbed me tighter.

Even better, I thought.

We ventured a little deeper still, and I felt her legs wrap tightly around me.

Maybe a little forward of her, but hey, whatever, I thought.

I could feel her heart pounding. My feet could now barely touch the sand between the swells, and she literally started shimmying herself up my body like she was climbing a tree.

This. Is. Awesome! I thought.

It was only later that I learned she could hardly swim. She swam like a brick is more like it, and her heart was pounding because she was absolutely terrified. As she climbed up my body to keep her head above water, she became deathly afraid she was going to drown me, which would also cause her ultimate demise. If I had drowned, it would have been totally worth it.

Despite the fact that she swam like a golf club, which has since been remedied, we continued to travel back and forth to see each other. We dated for all of seven months before I asked her to marry me while on a picnic at a beach near San Diego, where I had received orders shortly after we met when I finished flight school. That was September. We got married in December the same year.

I've always thought long engagements were a bit strange. I

mean, you should already be sure of your decision when you ask someone to marry you, and she should be sure when she says yes. At that point, you're both sure of the decision you're making together, confident that you want to spend the rest of your lives together and presumably ready for the plunge. So what's the point in waiting? Get yourselves some premarital counseling, plan the wedding, and get 'er done! I never understood why people stay engaged for a year or more. Weddings don't take that long to plan. Seriously, they don't. You need a pastor, your family, and a bride and groom. That's it! We humans overcomplicate things.

So what's with these super-long engagements? Are you giving yourself enough time to change your mind? Are you not really sure he's the one for you? If that's the case, don't get engaged! If you're not sure and you need more time to be sure, don't say yes! There's a great opportunity to get to know someone better within a mutually committed relationship without the full-blown commitment to marriage. It's called dating. Be boyfriend/girlfriend for a little while longer. Then if you don't feel like you could say yes if he asked you or if you don't know that you'd really want to shell out a couple grand for a ring for her, pull the plug, and do it fast. The engagement period is not for determining if you are compatible. That should already be settled. You are just making your life harder when you agree to get married and then don't set a date or set a date so far in the future that you have to scroll for thirteen minutes on the calendar on your phone just to get to it. Oh, and that whole "waiting 'til marriage to have sex" thing? That gets *a lot* harder when you're engaged. Just do it. Get married, I mean. Not *it*.

When I asked my wife to marry me, I knew I was ready and we could be happy together. She was everything I was looking for in a girl. Smart. Check. Beautiful. Check. A heart for God. Check. Independent. Check. Laughs at my jokes. We're still working on that. Excellent swimmer. Well, nobody's perfect. Poodle. Okay, if I'd learned about Charlie before she lured me in with her siren song or if I'd known he would try to bite me every night for the rest of my life, it probably would have been a deal-breaker. I would have wound up marrying someone with a hunting dog, like an English setter, a Lab, or Brittany spaniel. Something dignified and functional. Ah well. I'll overlook that one.

I'm certain I was everything she was looking for too. Brilliant. Check. Hilarious. Check. Hairy-knuckled, chest-pounding man's man. Check. A pillar of emotional stability and objectivity. Double-check. Humbleness that is exceeded only by devilish good looks. Check. Sensitive. No girl *really* wants that anyway. Artsy. If banging rocks together to make fire is artsy, then call me Picasso. Yep, she pretty much won the lottery.

All joking aside, poodle or no poodle, I knew she was right for me. So we did some counseling (an absolute must before you get married), planned the wedding (fast), and got hitched. Everything was perfect. And by that, I mean I could care less what kind of centerpieces were on the table at the reception, how the food tasted, or if anyone even showed up. I don't even remember what we served at the reception, aside from the fact that there was cake of some sort. You won't spend the rest of your married life thinking about your wedding. You likely won't even watch the video but once or twice. You won't have time to care what other people thought about the décor because you'll be married and you'll have your whole lives ahead of you. The wedding is just the beginning.

Plan Your Marriage, Not Your Wedding

I'm convinced that, if people spent half as much time and intentionality planning their marriage as they do planning their wedding, we would have far fewer marital issues today. Weddings are lots of fun, and I understand their importance. We should pause and recognize big decisions and commitments in our lives, and marriage is the biggest for most people. The wedding ceremony is full of symbolism and purpose—the exchanging of rings and vows as well as the giving away of the bride. They are beautiful and necessary. Above all, it's two people who decide to forego their old lives apart and do life together, to honor and serve one another. They make this commitment publicly in front of God and their closest friends and family, both to share their decision with them and to enlist their help and support along the way.

And of course, all major milestones should be celebrated. The reception to commemorate a man and a woman's fresh new life together is right. It's an acknowledgement and celebration of the step that was just taken. But I was ready for mine to be over before it ever started. Why? Well first of all, I simply dislike being the center of attention. I love seeing friends and family, of course, but I was ready to get out of there. I had a hot new bride waiting for me! But most of all, I just wanted to be married. I was ready and excited to get started, to share my life with someone else and start not just a new chapter of my life but a new volume entirely.

All too often, I see the wedding ceremony itself usurp the very reason for its existence. I watch as people's time, resources, and effort are poured into planning every detail of what amounts to a few hours of their lives. These are an important few hours, I agree. But you know what's not that important? Centerpieces. Centerpieces are not important. That and about a hundred other things.

It's okay to want to be married someday. It's even okay to want a big, huge, fancy wedding, if that's your thing. But let's not get bogged down in the details and lose sight of the bigger picture. Centerpieces can be very nice and tasteful, and everyone knows they *have* to match the flowers. But they won't aid your marriage in any way, and they certainly won't prevent you from getting divorced. Instead spend at least as much time planning your marriage as you spend planning your wedding. I promise you that your marriage will last far longer than your wedding.

How do you plan your marriage? It starts long before you even get engaged, before you meet your significant other, and long before you go wading out into the surf together. It starts with knowing who you are and who you were called to be. It builds on those periods of mindful singleness, in finding security and identity in God. And it grows by guarding your heart against superficial temptations and living a life according to God's will. Everything up to this point becomes a vital part of planning the marriage you want to have. But once you finally find the right person to do life with, planning your marriage takes on a more intentional and active role.

Ask the Hard Questions

Before she is given the opportunity to say yes, you hopefully already know the answers to a few very important questions. It's important to note that the answers to these questions will likely change over the course of your marriage, but discussing them ahead of time is essential. Here are just a few:

- Do you want children? How many? If you have grand images of a big, chaotic household with twelve kids crawling around, making messes, swinging from the chandelier, and loving every minute of it, now's the time to bring it up.

- When do you want to start having kids? Do you want a few years of marital bliss before learning how to change diapers, or are you ready to dive right in while you're still young?

- Where do you want to live? Would you move to advance someone's career? Do you want to stay close to family? Whose family?

- What are your favorite holiday traditions? How do you expect them to play out in your home? Will you decorate your house with multicolored lights, or are you a white-lights-only person? One of the first arguments my wife and I ever had was about Christmas lights. I just assumed everyone loved Christmas trees with multicolored lights. "White lights are dull." "What? Colored lights are tacky!" "Are you crazy?!" It sounds silly, but these traditions that have been ingrained in us from a young age become very important to us. There will be many surprises, but get the big stuff out of the way ahead of time.

- What are some things about your parents' marriage that you really love? What are some things about their relationship you want to do differently? And what about their relationship can't you stand? For most of us, the only example of marriage we get to see close up is our parents'. It's a mistake to assume your partner's parents do things the same way as your own. And your relationship, whether you like it or not, will not be exactly like theirs.

- Do you subscribe to traditional marital roles, or does the thought of staying home to feed babies while your husband leaves the cave to hunt make you sick to your stomach?

This list is by no means comprehensive. These are just a few of the things you should have already discussed while dating to determine whether or not you are compatible with each other. If you are dating someone with the end goal of pursuing marriage, these questions shouldn't be intimidating. At the heart of these questions is one thing: what your vision is for your future marriage. It's important to find someone who shares a similar vision for your future together.

Be Real

If you are going to spend the rest of your life with someone, he will eventually figure out that you were never really that into football, you actually hate running even though you joined a running club to spend more time with him while you were dating, and you absolutely despise his favorite shirt that he wears all the time. And you can only pretend for so long before she finally realizes that you are just feigning interest in her love of books, you hate all cats, especially *her* cats, and her mom drives you completely nuts. Love makes you a lot of things, but don't let it make you a liar.

Planning your marriage means being real because your opinions matter, and building a relationship founded on lies is like building a sand castle on the beach. All it takes is one big wave to wash it all away. When you are in the deep throes of love, your ability to overlook all those things that might make you cringe if they were said or done by a lesser person is quite remarkable. But the best gift you could ever give your boyfriend or girlfriend is the gift of being completely genuine with him or her. Your true colors will come to light eventually. Your significant other better see the real you before you say "I do."

The thought of being real should never frighten you. If you think someone can't love you for who you are, that you have to pretend to be someone you're not in order to be attractive, you are misguided. It should be just as troubling to you as it is to the person you're dating to think that this person might not truly love the real you. Remember, true intimacy is about revealing yourself completely to someone else, flaws and all, and being accepted. You can never achieve true intimacy without revealing yourself completely. Plan your marriage by ensuring that you're bringing your whole self to the table.

Seek Counsel

Premarital counseling is an absolute necessity before you get married. There is no substitute for the wise counsel of an experienced couple. You may think you've asked each other all the hard questions, but someone who has been married for a while will bring a unique perspective to your future marriage. A good counselor will force upon you the subjects you've managed to avoid and help you work through the areas where you might not have found alignment. A counselor will be able to bring out all of those expectations you have but haven't voiced yet. Once you put a ring on it, your next phone call (after your mother, of course) should be to your pastor to schedule your first session. That's how important it is.

Happily Ever After

What have you been planning for so long? Once all the flowers have wilted and the centerpieces have been thrown in the dumpster, what remains is your marriage. There are many people who have some very wrong, fairy-tale-like misperceptions about marriage and have absolutely no idea what they're asking for. Like I said before, they see marriage as a finish line and expect that, once they cross it, their lives will be perfectly complete, lacking nothing. Oh, how far this is from the truth.

But before we get to what lies ahead in marriage, I want to dispel a significant marriage misconception that I see infiltrating the minds of many. As I alluded to before, happily ever after is a myth, a fairy tale, a phrase coined by a head-in-the-clouds dreamer. If you are looking forward to your wedding day because you can't wait to begin your "happily ever after," you are setting yourself up for disappointment. Marriage is not a magic pill that will make you happy. If you are unhappy before you're married, I'm not sure that marriage is going to change that. If you are putting your faith in a person rather than God to complete you, you will never feel complete.

Don't get me wrong. Marriage can be fun, exciting, and wonderful. But it takes work for it to be great. It takes personal sacrifice for it to be great. That means you may have to give up something good, something you love, and something you've always done so you can achieve something better together. Marriage isn't easy, despite what you may think. Your marriage must be watered, pruned, fed, and nurtured. Yes, you should marry someone who is easy for you to love because there will be times when loving him or her will get a lot harder. Two lovebirds at the altar generally have no concept of the hardships they'll have to face together. When they hear, "For richer, for poorer, in sickness and in health, for better, for worse," often, up to this point, all that they've experienced is the better, richer, and healthy part of that equation. But in the pastor's wisdom, he slips in a little taste of what's to come.

If you need some help imagining what happily ever after truly looks like, let me give you some ideas. Happily ever after is getting to know someone completely and loving them despite their imperfections. It's Saturday nights spent snuggled on the couch together while watching a movie. It's working long hours, earning money to put the other through school. It's sacrificing your own promising career for someone else's. It's fighting over the same silly thing again. It's making beautiful plans together. It's struggling to conceive, month after month, year after year. It's fertility treatments, miscarriage, and disappointment. It's not understanding why children come so easily for others and not for you. It's questioning God. It's celebrating milestones, anniversaries, promotions, graduations, and new careers. It's mourning unexpected loss. It's the joy of receiving the child you always wanted. It's tee-ball games, soccer games, and pouring yourself into raising children. It's being blindsided by a child with an unexpected need who requires a very different, special kind of love, one you didn't even know you had the capacity for. It's rediscovering the spark you let fade amidst the busyness of life. It's the stress of moving again, losing a job, making life-changing decisions, and being unsure of where they might take you. It's high expectations, plans, and dreams. It's failure and forgiveness. Hope and restoration. Through it all, it's a partner who would rather deal with your problems and your special brand of crazy than anyone else's. That's what happily ever after looks like.

Not Enough

The description above may not be what you thought of when you first heard the phrase "and they lived happily ever after" at the end of a fairy tale. No one goes into a marriage expecting to get divorced, yet so many people end up that way. I think this is due, at least in part, to our fairy-tale culture that has given us inflated expectations of love and marriage. We've painted ourselves too rosy a picture, where the lows are silly misunderstandings and the highs are unattainable hogwash. We go into relationships bringing what we thought was enough and quit at the realization that what is truly required of us far exceeds what we had imagined. We quit when we realize what we gave wasn't enough.

Love Is Not Enough

We want to believe that love is always enough. We want to believe that love prevails, that what we're feeling when we say "I do" is somehow powerful enough to get us through the hardest times. Yes, love is required, but it is not enough. We only have one word for love in the English language, so I better unpack what I mean when I say that love is not enough.

It's not enough to harbor the strong feeling of affection, attraction, and desire for another person who fully reciprocates those feelings back toward you. This type of love is strong. It can cover a multitude of sins. But it can also grow weary if not properly attended to.

To say that love conquers all is poetic and comforting, but you won't find it in the Bible. The closest you'll come is in Romans 8:37, "We are more than conquerors through him who loved us." Though if you read this passage in context, I think you'll find that it pertains to overcoming suffering and persecution rather than marriage. (However, if your marriage feels like a persecution, maybe you can draw strength from it.) The love referred to in this passage is also

God's love for us, not our love for others. God's love surely conquers all. After all, His love has already won. But to say that our human love, more specifically the love for your spouse, conquers all is only true insofar as we love like Jesus. If we all loved like Jesus all the time, surely it would be enough. But alas, this is not so. We need Jesus precisely because we *don't* always love like Him.

We tend to worship love in our culture, but love can also be easily misplaced. To say that God is love is true, but to say that love is God is a grave mistake. If we let it, love, absent from God, becomes an idol. In *The Four Loves*, C. S. Lewis says this about love, "But [love], honoured without reservation and obeyed unconditionally, becomes a demon." And later, "The couple whose marriage will certainly be endangered by them, and possibly ruined, are those who have idolized [love] ... We must do the works of [love] when [love] is not present."[4]

Love is required in any healthy marriage, but if we are to exhibit the type of love Paul wrote about to the Corinthians, the patient, kind, unselfish kind of love, we must learn to worship the source of love, not love itself. If we allow ourselves to overly romanticize it to such a point that we think love alone will save us or allow ourselves to believe that love without action is enough, we will find ourselves worshiping at the altar of love, our god, and standing by the wayside as it gets smothered by the very life we thought we wanted.

Yes, we must do the works of love when love is absent, when the emotion is lost in the throes of a fight or diluted by day-to-day strife. "If you love those who love you, what credit is that to you? Even sinners love those who love them" (Luke 6:32). When you are full of affection and desire for one another, the works of love follow easily. When affection and desire are lost, it is carrying out the works of love that will lead you back to the affection and desire that once came so easily.

---

[4] C. S. Lewis, *The Four Loves*, (New York: Harcourt Brace, 1960), 110, 114-115.

It's Not Enough That You're Both Christians

If you think that your marriage is bound to succeed by the mere fact that you are both Christians, you are wrong. It is a good start, for sure, to be devoted to God first and devoted to your spouse second. In so keeping, I do believe you'll find strength in your marriage far beyond the norm. And yet Christians still get divorced. Why? Why is it so hard to remain steadfastly devoted to your spouse?

In my early days flying in the navy, I feared failure. This fear was not just a fear of washing out of flight school, though that too would weigh on my mind, but a fear that I might do something stupid, forget my procedures, and "ball one up," as they say. Sure, if I were lucky, I'd walk away uninjured, though unlikely to fly again. But if I were unlucky, if I really messed up, they'd be scraping me off the runway with a shovel. In retrospect, a little fear was a good motivator.

Becoming a good pilot requires a great deal of discipline, hard work, careful study, sound judgment, and experience. Maybe even a little talent too. It's hard to pick any one of these things and single it out as the most important, but it's clear that experience is very highly valued in the community. This is likely because it's the only one of these traits that is quantifiable. Experience for a pilot is measured in flight hours. More flight hours means more experience. More clout. These hours are coveted and competed for, and they are a source of pride in any squadron. As a helicopter pilot, you can't even be considered for the aircraft commander designation, the person who is responsible for the conduct and safety of the aircraft and its crew, until you reach five hundred hours.

Experience, however, is a double-edged sword. There is a range of flight hours known as "the complacency zone," which, generally speaking, runs somewhere between 500 and 1,500 flight hours. In this zone, more flight mishaps occur that can be directly attributed to human error. In this zone, the training wheels are off, and you know just enough to be dangerous. It's where experience breeds overconfidence. It's here where you might start to set aside your old study habits, where you've experienced enough situations to feel comfortable, and where that healthy fear begins to fade. It's here where that feeling of comfort, the empowering feeling of confidence, must be intentionally tempered, lest complacency corrupt it. If you're not careful, it's in this zone when you begin to feel comfortable in situations where you should feel uncomfortable.

The complacency zone. If you are not careful, it too can creep up in your marriage and your spiritual life. After you've been married for a while, life begins to overtake you, and you stop doing the things you once did. You used to study your spouse, talk to each other late into the night, schedule time for each other, and go on dates. Maybe you used to feel a little uncomfortable when that coworker would flirt with you, but now you see it as flattering, exciting, and fun. Perhaps you used to go to church with a heart full of worship, but now, if you actually make it there on Sunday, you find yourself just going through the motions. After all, you have kids now, and getting everyone there on time is a real pain.

Complacency does not discriminate. It doesn't care if you're a Christian, if you truly love each other, how long you dated, how long you've been married, or how many kids you have. It doesn't care how much experience you have. This is why simply being a Christian is not enough to keep your marriage together. Complacency can creep into any marriage, subtly luring you into a false sense of security. There is nothing wrong with being comfortable. Your marriage should feel comfortable. But complacency fools you into being comfortable in situations when you should feel uncomfortable.

When you were dating, you used to pick up on those subtle cues your partner exhibited that told you something wasn't quite right. You were alert to them, and they led you to action. They compelled you to ask, "What's wrong?" And instead of getting angry or offended at the response, the response motivated you to do something, even if it meant going out of your way or making a sacrifice. Complacency blinds you to the signals you used to pick up. Or worse, it makes you indifferent to them.

The best lies go unsaid. They lurk just below the surface, disguised as assumptions. In this regard, complacency is one of the best liars of all. It tells you that the achievements of yesterday are good enough for today. The things you used to do for your husband should be enough for him to know that you still love him. You used to be intentional about your faith. You used to be intentional with prayer. You used to go to church every Sunday. That should be enough, right? That you used to do these things should be enough for you to continue to think of yourself as a strong, faithful Christian wife or husband. It's enough to make you *feel* comfortable.

Can you still be a Christian if you never go to church? Perhaps so. But I think there's a reason God tells us to set aside one day a week for Him. He created us after all, and He knows how we operate. He knows that, if our values don't dictate our habits, then our habits will eventually dictate our values. He knows that faith without fruit saves only yourself and perhaps not even that. When we build up habits that don't reflect the faith we proclaim, then simply being a Christian will not be enough to make your marriage work.

Loving someone may be the hardest thing you will ever do. It takes more than we ever thought we had to give. Sometimes it takes everything we have. Love is a verb. Love without action ceases to be love at all. And love without sacrifice is a marriage without intimacy. When I look at the sacrifices my wife has made for me, I don't see resentment or regret. I see love. When she left her family, her friends, and her home state behind to follow me, I saw love. When she moved with me from state to state, enduring long deployments for the sake of my career, I saw love. When she gave me four beautiful children, sacrificing her youthful body for their development and her time for their nourishment and sustainment, I saw love. Love speaks the language of sacrifice. To borrow from Lewis, love whispers in your pleasure, comforts in your pain, but shouts in your sacrifice.

If you want a marriage that lasts, you must go beyond love that manifests itself solely as affection and desire because the affection you felt yesterday can turn to resentment tomorrow if it is not put into action today. Likewise, you can't rely on the faith you had yesterday to guide you through the tough times without practicing it and allowing yourself to be filled by it, day after day.

If there's one thing I can drive home with this chapter, it's that getting married is not the end. It's the beginning. It's important that you set realistic expectations for yourself in marriage. That's why I cringe when I hear advice to young girls that focuses on finding *the one* and achieving your "happily ever after," as if life is a fairy tale. What follows the scene where the carriage carries off the prince and princess, with the "Just Married" sign hanging behind it, are the words "The End."

Nothing could be further from the truth. It's not as if the advice I see and read about boys and girls and dating and relationships is bad necessarily. It's just dangerously incomplete. The advice you hear may very well encourage you to avoid mistakes, make good decisions, and find the right person to marry. However, I fear that, once married, problems will arise because of unmet and unrealistic expectations. I desperately want to see marriages succeed. I want you to experience love, intimacy, joy, and happiness in the confines of a healthy, stable marriage. It is possible.

But know that the love you feel and the faith you share when you are standing there together at the altar didn't just happen. You allowed it to happen. You made it happen. And it will fade unless you continue to make it happen and refuse to let complacency take up residence in your marriage.

Love is a choice you make every day, not a feeling that will naturally last forever. Hardship will find you, and if you are tempted to rely on yesterday's love and yesterday's faith to carry you through these times, you'll likely find that what once was enough is no longer sufficient.

Building a marriage is like building a house. Your love, your faith, your history, your experience, and the habits you form as you build relationships that guide your heart to the right person will form the foundation. A strong foundation is critical to success, and a foundation is what you have when you get married. Your home is what you build after that. No one finishes a foundation, rolls out a sleeping bag, and resides there. When the winds blow and the storms come, there's nothing to protect you from the sleet and hail that will surely follow. No, you continue building, brick by brick, until the walls go up and the roof takes shape. Now when the storms come, you are protected, not because of love or luck, but because of the hard work you poured into the construction.

Still, a big enough storm can come crashing through, ripping the roof right off your house. But it's okay because you still have a strong foundation and four walls still standing. Now you have a hard choice: rebuild or walk away. Rebuilding will take all of your time, resources, sweat, and strength, but it'll be worth it and leave your house stronger than it was before.

Even when finished, your house needs constant attention. The plants need to be watered, shutters painted, and leaks fixed. There is a house just down the street from my neighborhood that is a total disaster. The lawn is a mess with weeds, grass, trees, and bushes that have been ignored and allowed to take over. The walls are cracked. The roof is pitted with holes. Mountains of garbage, tinged with rust, are piled high all over the yard. It has seen years, maybe even decades, of neglect. My house, though it bears little resemblance to my neighbor's down the street, does share one thing in common with this dilapidated mess. Both were new once. At some point, someone carefully built that house and worked hard on it. Beginning with a foundation, someone poured their own sweat into its construction with dedication until it was complete.

What happened after that is anyone's guess. Perhaps those who built it thought the hard work was finally behind them. Maybe something unexpected happened, and the roof caved in. And begrudgingly, instead of putting the effort into rebuilding, they threw up a tarp instead. The next time something happened, they just patched it up again with a little duct tape or maybe just left it the way it was out of resentment. After all, they had already built their house. This wasn't supposed to happen. It was not in their plans.

The envy of every neighborhood is the house that has it all together. It's that beautiful one on the corner with soft red brick with stone accent. It has beautifully crafted landscaping and grass so green that it looks like you could toss it in a salad. What you don't see are the hours spent in the garden, trimming trees, pruning hedges, planting flowers, painting, fixing, and replacing. That beautiful house didn't just happen, and neither does a healthy marriage.

If you find yourself years down the road looking at someone else's marriage and thinking to yourself, *I wish I had that*, then maybe it's time you step back and look at your own marriage. Ask yourself how you got there. What weeds need to be pulled? What repairs have been neglected? What has been left unsaid and undone for far too long? What did it *used* to look like when it was new, before life happened? What do you *want* it to look like now? And how do you get there? One thing is certain. It won't happen by itself.

When it comes to marriage, coming together is just the beginning. It is what you build after that that truly determines whether or not your marriage is successful. It is my prayer for you that, if and when you find the right person to build a life with, you will enjoy many, many years of growth together.

CHAPTER 13
Lessons to Live By

Show me your faith without deeds, and I will show
you my faith by my deeds.

—James 2:18

You learn many things as you experience life and see how others
react differently to similar situations. I watch adults all the
time who never seem to figure life out, where every obstacle is
insurmountable and overwhelming for them and opportunities are
passed up out of fear or misunderstanding. I see people who seem
not to have learned even the most basic lessons of life.

I know it's not for me to judge. Perhaps they were left a bad
example to follow or had no example at all. Maybe they have a
struggle that I just can't understand, a thorn in their side that's
completely invisible to me. But whether you had the best role
models in the world or role models who were the epitome of failure,
you can take something away from the truths that follow.

Embrace Failure

For though the righteous fall seven times, they rise
again. (Proverbs 24:16)

One of the biggest personal setbacks I've experienced was when I was a young pilot at my first squadron. I was a mere copilot when I sat down to take the test to become an aircraft commander. I say test, but this wasn't a pencil and paper–style exam. It was a board of six or seven experienced pilots who, as I sat down in front of them, bombarded me with questions. Everything I'd learned in the years leading up to that point was fair game: rules, regulations, aircraft systems, and emergency procedures. It was all on the table. Foremost among these questions were scenarios that often incorporated them all. For hours, they would present scenario after scenario and ask how I would respond. What would you do in this situation if you experienced an emergency? Would you land? Where would you land? Would you continue with the mission? What if someone were dying in the back of your helicopter and needed to get to a hospital? Would that change your mind? Would you be willing to risk the lives of your copilot and crew to save that one person? What if the weather started deteriorating? What would you do? How would you do it? Would you break the rules in order to complete the mission?

Talk about stressful. But that was the point. The point was not simply to judge my knowledge of the helicopter and procedures. As a copilot, I should already know that stuff. The point was to judge my ability to assess the scenario and make a good decision in a stressful but realistic environment. Anyone can fly a plane when the weather is great and everything is behaving perfectly. It's when things go wrong, when the unexpected happens, that a skilled, competent person is required to make the tough calls.

This exam was, in effect, a system designed to judge my judgment. In so doing, they would press hard. Once I made a decision, someone would try to talk me out of it and get me to change my mind, to second-guess myself. They wanted to know if I could make a decision and stick to it. In aviation, being indecisive can be just as bad or worse than making a bad decision.

When I finally stepped out of that room and left the members of the board to decide my fate, I felt exhausted, stressed, frustrated, and uneasy. I knew I had done poorly, a sentiment that would be confirmed to me thirty minutes later when they invited me back in to debrief my performance.

Failing is never easy, and it's never fun. Sometimes it just plain stinks. Yes, it has its benefits, but at the time, no one wants to hear how failure will be good for them. It takes a little time to look back on your failure to fully see how it changed you for the better. But it does one thing almost immediately. It forces you to question yourself. It draws you to introspection.

When I lay down in my rack on the ship that night, after failing one of the most important steps in my progression as a pilot, I was flooded with self-doubt. Did I make a mistake in doing this? Should I have chosen a different career path for myself? Do I really have what it takes to be a good pilot?

Failure draws from us a deep honesty that we seldom see otherwise. It gives us a double helping of something many of us desperately need: humility. From this position of humility, we can truly see the world around us with clarity. Through the lens of humility, we are better able to empathize with others instead of seeing others as less than ourselves.

When I say that you should welcome failure, not only does that mean you should learn from it, you should invite it. You'll never fail if you never try. Basketball legend Michael Jordan gave this synopsis of his career, "I've missed more than nine thousand shots in my career. I've lost almost three hundred games. Twenty-six times, I've been trusted to take the game-winning shot and missed. I've failed over and over and over again in my life. And that is why I succeed." Successful people understand that, in taking risks, sticking your neck out, and opening the door for failure, we truly open the door for ourselves to succeed. You can't be successful without inviting failure. You can't make shots you don't take.

Maybe you've seen all kinds of success in school or work and you've never really experienced failure. To that, I'll say that perhaps you are playing it too safe. You may be the smartest, most talented person on the planet, but if you haven't failed, you likely haven't stretched yourself far enough yet. Don't play it safe. Don't be afraid to make tough decisions. We are often faced with opportunities that present themselves as something that could be great, but only if we're brave enough to step away from the safety and familiarity of our lives. The choice then becomes: do you step outside the comfortable, familiar life you've made for yourself, or do you continue cruising down the safe and shallow glide path you're already on? In this case, no decision is a decision to let an opportunity pass you by. It's a decision to avoid failure. It could also be a decision to avoid tremendous success, to avoid your full potential, and to avoid the rewards that are set aside for the bravest among us.

Failure isn't helpful if you don't let it shape and direct you. In other words, if you don't learn from it, if failure causes you to retreat instead of advance, then you have let it win. Don't let it win. Learn from it. Then keep going.

Some of the biggest successes came from failure. There's a term in the business start-up world that sums up what it means to fail, learn, change, and adapt, in that order. It's called a pivot. When a company is started with a specific vision in mind and every resource and minute of time is poured into making that vision a reality, only to find that consumers don't want what they're selling, two choices exist: close shop or adapt and change. Sometimes when a company is on the verge of failure, they'll recognize that the few people who are using their product are using it in a very different and unexpected way. When this occurs, they can look at this unintended insight, and if they accept that their original plan was a failure, they can pivot from being a company that produced something no one wanted to become a company that focuses on what's succeeding rather than what's failing.

A small tech company started years ago with the intention of becoming a podcast platform. Around the same time, a much bigger, more recognizable, and established company called Apple announced that they would use their existing iTunes software as a podcasting platform and build it into every one of the millions of iPods they had already sold. This meant "game over" for this little tech startup. They had to change and change fast. So they did. They pivoted from being a podcast company to a status update company, and you know them today as Twitter.

There is plenty to learn from failure. But learning to push through, to press on, to advance when retreating would be so much easier, to get back up and keep going despite all the games lost, shots missed, and giants who stand ready to crush you, that's a skill that no one can teach you except failure. And he's eager to do it. If you find yourself failing often, don't be discouraged. To fail presupposes you had the courage to try, and to fail often simply means you are braver than most and you've already learned to let your setbacks propel you forward. Turn your set*backs* into set*forwards*. Let failure shape you, and learn to recognize when it's time to get back up or to pivot into something new so at least you never fail the same way twice.

A couple of months after failing my first board, I had the opportunity to step back into that room, to learn from my mistakes, and to silence the doubts in my mind. This time I passed, but that, of course, wasn't the end. Now those fictitious scenarios were mine to struggle through in real life. The same weaknesses I exhibited in my first exam—my indecision and lack of confidence—were still there with me. But with each decision I made in that aircraft, I gained experience. With each flight, I gained confidence. Each new scenario that hit me was the *last* time I'd face that situation for the *first* time because I learned and carried those lessons forward. Eventually after hours of hard work and experience, I would arrive at a place in my career where my weaknesses didn't appear so weak to an outsider. It didn't happen overnight. It was slogged out in the trenches. It came through setbacks, pain, uncertainty, and failure. It came through facing each of these head-on and always, always pressing forward.

Life Isn't Fair

> The poor and the oppressor have this in common:
> The Lord gives sight to the eyes of both. (Proverbs
> 29:13)

This will be a very unpopular lesson at this time in our society. There's almost no greater sin today than that of offending someone else with your ideas that run counter to theirs. Everything today must be 100 percent equal, without even a hint of being otherwise, lest we are called to fall upon our swords and repent for this grave sin or even the mere perception of it. Our society worships at the altar of equality because apparently there is no greater god than the god of fairness.

"Repent," they cry. "Repent for your privilege, for being born with more than someone else. Repent for your parents who had the gall to lift you up and help you to succeed. Repent for the zip code you grew up in with its Starbucks, Whole Foods Markets, hot yoga studios, and country clubs."

The self-righteousness in these cries is unnerving first and foremost because they too are attempting to achieve that which they shout against. Yes, perhaps you earned what others were given. But you did so first for yourself and second so your children would have more opportunity than you had, so they would have the privilege of standing on your shoulders to reach higher than you did. Yes, it took you longer. Yes, you had to work harder—and all so your children won't have to work as hard or as long as you did.

There is no need to apologize for how you grew up or who your parents are. "From everyone who has been given much, much will be demanded; and from the one who has been entrusted with much, much more will be asked" (Luke 12:48). God acknowledges that life isn't fair. It is right to acknowledge the help we've had on our way, but no one needs apologize for it, just as no one needs apologize for being born with less. But it is surely wrong to discredit those on the bottom rung as fools, squanderers, or less deserving. Who provided your riches? Who provided your privilege? Luke implies that it wasn't you. He implies that God has entrusted you and so you've been given much. And for this reason, more will be asked of you than those who have been given little.

I'm not saying anything about where we are as a society or even where we need to go with respect to equality. What I'm saying is that life isn't fair, and the sooner you acknowledge that, the sooner we can all move on. No, it's not fair that one child is born into poverty while another is born rich. It's not fair that one child is born to two loving parents while another is born into a broken home. It's not fair that one child is born with disabilities she will struggle with her entire life while another is born completely healthy. These things are beyond our control, and we would do well to spend less time dwelling on them.

My son cannot take anything that seems unfair. He will call me out if I don't do exactly what I said I would do. If I spend just a minute or two longer tucking his sister into bed than I spend with him, he will cry foul. That's to be expected from a seven-year-old. But some people never grow out of this.

Jesus didn't seem at all concerned with the inequality of society as a whole. That seems very strange to say right now, but it's true. He didn't spend His time on earth attempting to break down the hierarchy of the Roman empire and establishing a new, more fair system of governance. It's funny because that is exactly what the Jews thought the Messiah would do. He was to be king, to establish His kingdom on earth. But that's not what happened. He didn't come to change the laws of man. The most political He got was "give back to Caesar what is Caesar's and to God what is God's" (Mark 12:17). Instead He came to change the one thing that truly matters, our hearts.

When asked what the greatest commandment in the law was, Jesus replied, "'Love the lord your God with all your heart and with all your soul and with all your mind.' This is the first and greatest commandment. And the second is like it: 'love your neighbor as yourself.' All the law and the prophets hang on these two commandments" (Matthew 22:37–40). That's His answer to inequality.

In story after story, we see Jesus demonstrate how to love our neighbor. The Good Samaritan shows us the extent to which we should go to love those in need, though they do not belong to our social group. He demonstrated this love when He ate with sinners and healed those who had been cast out of society. But I think the most poignant example of this mind-set is in John 9 when He and His disciples come across a man blind from birth and His disciples asked, "Rabbi, who sinned, this man or his parents, that he was born blind?" (John 9:2). Two thousand years later, we still don't get this right.

We read this and think, *How silly that they thought a person was born blind because of his parents' sin or even his own. Clearly they have no understanding of science.* And yet we make this same assumption every single day when we look on the homeless and the needy with judgment in our hearts instead of compassion. How often have you refused to give a beggar the change in your pocket because you thought quietly to yourself that he would use it to buy drugs or booze? He would squander it, you assume. *I could make much better use of it,* you think.

But what we are really doing is making the same assumption the disciples made. We state with resounding inaction that this man is here because of his sin. Or if we have a little more compassion, we assume that it's not completely his fault. Maybe he had bad parents who didn't instill our traditional Western values in him. Two thousand years of progress and our response is exactly the same as the disciples. Who sinned? This man or his parents that he finds himself on the streets?

Jesus's response to them before healing the man is unexpected. "'Neither this man nor his parents sinned,' said Jesus, 'but this happened so that the works of God might be displayed in him'" (John 9:3). This should come across as shocking to us for two reasons. First, it's a slap in the face to our self-righteous judgment. The man isn't blind because of sin. He's there so Jesus can heal him, so the works of God might be displayed in him.

Think about that the next time you see someone in need. Let that sink in when a man asks you for some change and your first impulse is to reject him, to cast him out as an unworthy sinner. You know nothing of his past, but in your own mind, there's no other explanation for his current situation. He must be lazy. He must be a squanderer. They're all addicts. You'd be doing him more harm than good if you gave him a little money. And without the slightest knowledge of his present circumstances, we walk away, keeping our hope and our faith and our hearts tucked firmly away in our wallets where, we assume, they deserve to be.

But maybe that person was placed there not so you could judge him, but so that the works of God might be displayed in him through *you*. After all, we are His hands and feet, right? Are we not the body of Christ? Do we not believe it is more blessed to give than to receive? Or is it only to those we think are deserving of our blessing that we're called to give? Whoa to us all if God felt the same way.

The second thing to take away might be even more shocking. "This happened so the works of God might be displayed in him." Are we to assume from this that God caused this man's blindness? That He allowed it to happen? Is there a difference? This man had lived his entire life unable to see. How fair is that? If you had lived your entire life without ever being able to see your own parents, the beauty of a sunset, or the physical obstacles in your way, only to be healed by God and told you were blind all those years only so He could demonstrate His power, what would be your response?

I think that today many people's response would be one of anger. "You mean I could have seen my whole life were it not for your plan? I forfeited twenty years of sight, twenty years of stumbling, suffering, and begging, when I didn't have to? Couldn't you have shown your power through someone else? Through *something* else? I wouldn't have chosen this! *That's not fair!*" Yet this man's response when he finally sees Jesus for the first time through a blind man's eyes, is, "'Lord, I believe,' and he worshipped him" (John 9:38).

The world is not fair. God apparently is not fair. Jesus didn't come into the world to make it fair and equitable for all or to change our laws or system of government. He came to change our hearts. He understood that, if each one of us truly loved God and, in so doing, loved our neighbor, we would have no need for the governance and the laws of man because we would be operating under the laws of God, the law of grace. And through that, we bring heaven to earth.

Are there times to stand up for justice? Absolutely. But don't lose sight of the bigger picture. Laws can change and change right back. But a changed heart changes the world. We must accept that life isn't fair. It doesn't have to be. God has a plan and a purpose, whether we see it or remain blind.

Lose with Grace

> Before a downfall the heart is haughty, but humility comes before honor. (Proverbs 18:12)

Whenever we leave our house at an unexpected time, as we prepare to go, my stepdog becomes visibly nervous. He knows he likely won't be going with us and seems to realize when we leave that we aren't going to work and he therefore can't expect us to return at the usual time. So he paces and paws randomly at things, letting out a bark or whimper every now and then. He should know by now that we always come back, even if it is after dark. But still he paces.

Once we are gone, his anxiety takes over, and it stews and

festers into vindictive anger. In other words, he gets livid. If we happen to leave our bathroom door open, which seems to happen quite often, Charlie will go in there, dig through the trash can until he finds a few select items that smell like my wife, and carefully pull them out and shred them, leaving them displayed all over our bathroom and bedroom floor. It's not reckless or impulsive. It's a cold and calculated move. His marble-sized brain is firing on every tiny, inefficient cylinder to send us a carefully crafted message, "You left me, you mongrels!"

This story has no moral. It's just me venting about my crazy, ill-behaved dog-child. If we take him on walks, someone inevitably will comment on how cute he is, which is an adjective no man wants associated with his adult dog, and how they've heard how great poodles are as pets. They're just so smart. They're such great pets. It takes all of my willpower not to slap them in the face and walk away.

Here is a list of some of the annoying comments I get and the comments I *want* (and sometimes do) make in reply:

"Oh, how cute! Is she a puppy?"

"No. He's just an idiot."

"Look at the puppy! Can I pet him?"

"Not if you value your fingers."

"Look how adorable he is! I just wanna take him home!"

"Seriously? Don't say things you don't mean."

"Dude, your dog looks like a cat."

"Yes! Yes! Thank you! Someone gets it!"

Be aware. If you ever have the misfortune of seeing me walk my stepdog and have the nerve to tell me how cute he is, be prepared to receive a mouthful of curly black poodle fur as I scoop him up, shove him in your face, and hand you the leash as I run the other direction.

Well, I feel better after getting that out of my system. Now let's talk about how not to be a sore loser.

You may have already guessed it, but I'm a pretty good loser

153

most of the time. Maybe my abundant humility stems from the fact that my dog weighs less than a Happy Meal. Or perhaps it's because I've had a lot of practice at losing. I was a part of many losing teams growing up and only a handful of good ones. But the team that sticks out in my mind the most was my football team during my junior year of high school. We won a whopping two games that year, but that doesn't fully describe the misery of that season. Part of the reason we made a habit of losing was because our team was really made up of two teams: the seniors and everybody else.

The seniors lorded their seniority over the rest of us every day. They somehow felt anointed by their title, and rather than compelling them to lead, it somehow bestowed on them the right to treat us like their underlings. They might have pulled it off had they possessed the athletic talent to back up their reign of negativity. But unfortunately they weren't that big, strong, fast, or talented—although they thought they were.

Losing was all but in our blood that year. And with every mistake and missed opportunity, there were our very own teammates standing, ready to tear us down. The very leaders of the team were the first to complain, the first to cry foul, the first to rip someone apart for making a mistake. They would even tear each other down. No one was exempt from their criticism. We were good at one thing, losing. Come to think of it, we weren't even good at that. In the aftermath of each predictable defeat, there were throes, fits, and accusations, but a distinct lack of humility and grace.

Some people chalk up their bad behavior on the field to being extremely competitive. Being a sore loser is not the same as being competitive. Fierce competitors hate to lose. It's true, but shattering your racket on the clay of the court or throwing your helmet across the locker room in a fit of rage is not to be confused with being competitive. Being competitive means allowing the competitors around you to elevate your level of play. Being competitive is saying

"Again!" after your opponent bests you. It's what drives you to rise to the occasion rather than shrink from it. It does not dictate your behavior, no matter the outcome, after the match. The fiercest competitors can still lose with grace, shake your hand, and move on. But rest assured, when you meet again, they'll hold nothing back because they've been preparing for the rematch every day since the scoreboard told them they'd come just shy of victory.

One of the things I remember about that season is that our practice T-shirts said, "Expect to Win" in big, bold letters across the chest. Nothing could have been further from the truth. We had an expectation of failure, the onset of which came early in the season, though I can't pinpoint exactly when. We had a defeatist mind-set. Each game, we ran out onto the field like lemmings heading for a cliff. We weren't a team. There was no unifying voice or vision from the senior class worthy of following. There was no leadership. Their attitude was toxic. It infiltrated the entire team, right down to the bottom ranks.

Here's what happens when you never learn to lose with grace. First, you deny honor where it's due, like a child who whips the Monopoly board off the table at the realization that he or she has lost, denying the winner any recognition of victory by attempting to mask your own failure. Though the person on the other side of the field, court, or table might have worked hard to prepare and develop a winning strategy, executing it to perfection, by your attitude, you diminish the hard work the victor put in. No one wants to play against someone like that. And down the road, no one wants that person on their team, whether it's on the field or off.

When you never learn to lose with grace, you learn to make excuses. Losers always have a reason for losing. Maybe it was the official's fault for calling a bad game, the coach for pulling you out, a team that cheated, or a lucky shot. Perhaps your boss or teacher has it out for you. Maybe you are smarter than everyone else and everyone else is too dumb to realize it. If there's a reason, losers will find it. I'm not sure that group of seniors on my team ever owned our losses. I think they found blame everywhere else rather than acknowledging their own shortcomings. That is no way to walk through life.

To lose with grace, you must be able to admit to and acknowledge your own shortcomings. You must recognize that, on that particular day at that particular time, someone else fought just a little harder than you did. Someone else was better. Everyone loses at some point, whether it's a race, a game, a promotion that was given to someone else, or a person you thought would be yours who rejects you for someone else. Whatever it is, at some point, you'll taste the bitter taste of defeat. And how you react to that will say more about your character than all the victories in the world. It's easy to find grace when you're standing on the podium or when you're sipping champagne and digging your fork into the choicest steak as onlookers marvel at your success. But when that bitter cup is passed to you and you take a full, deep drink of defeat, how will you respond? Will you throw blame every which way? Toward your wife? Your boss? Your boyfriend? Your children? Your teachers? Will you cast a shadow on those who beat you, marginalizing their win? Will the setback propel you forward, or will you shrink from further responsibility, afraid to give it your best in fear that you might discover that your best isn't good enough?

I wish I could say that we turned things around the following year. I wish I could say that we rose to the occasion and stepped up to fill the chasm of leadership that was begging to be filled. But we still lost. It was all we knew how to do. But I will say this. We lost *better*. Though we couldn't quite shake the losing mind-set that had been drilled into our heads the previous year, we refused to cast a pall on ourselves. We had all experienced the ramifications of that, and we rejected it. We owned our losses. In doing so, we helped lift the veil of shame that hung over us. I'd like to think it was a turning point in the program. We couldn't change it all, and we couldn't win, but we could transform how we lost. And that was something worthy of passing on to the next generation.

Losing is sometimes unavoidable, but how you lose reveals your character. Lose with grace. Walk out with your head held high. Blame no one but yourself. Take ownership of the mistakes you make, and learn from them. Most importantly, shake the hand of whoever is better than you on that day. Look the person in the eye and say, "Well done." You may have lost, but you don't have to be a loser.

Ask for Help

A friend loves at all times, and a brother is born for a time of adversity. (Proverbs 17:17)

I am a rock. I am the epitome of stability. I'm unsinkable, unshakeable, and unbreakable. At least most of the time.

When I was growing up, my family used to take vacations frequently to Colorado. It was a favorite destination of ours. We would hike, bike, and explore the beauty and fullness of the mountains. On one occasion, when I was little, we traveled there during the winter with my cousins to go skiing. After the first full day of skiing, I remember piling into the back of my aunt's brand-new minivan, feeling completely and utterly exhausted. My head was aching. My body was weak from exertion and the physiological effects of the thin mountain air. I began to feel nauseous, and before I could make it out of the van, I leaned forward and threw up all over the floor of that brand-new car.

I love the mountains, but the altitude has just never agreed with me. Every time we traveled there, the first day I'd have a pounding headache. The second day, I would feel weak, with the weakness working its way through my body like a virus, culminating in the eventual but certain expulsion of the contents of my stomach. It was a persistent pattern, one that seemed to be unique to my physiology. The rest of my family was much less phased by the altitude sickness that plagued me.

I thought I might eventually grow out of that misery, and by the time I reached my late teens, it appeared that I had. We went back one summer after several years of being unable to go. I was looking forward to the trip but dreading the first two days. When we arrived, I stepped out of the car and smelled the familiar smell of the mountains. If that smell could be bottled up or stuffed into an overpriced candle, I would call it, "Nauseous Pine." It smells sweet, vast, wild, and beautiful, but also makes me want to throw up a little bit for obvious reasons. But on that trip, day one went by with only a mild albeit lingering headache. Day two, aside from the normal fatigue, came and went with the contents of my stomach remaining firmly in place. By day three, I was feeling fit as a mountain goat. Toward the end of that trip, having felt like I'd finally outgrown my altitude sickness, we decided to tackle a real challenge. No more petty hikes through the woods. No more cute little twelve thousand-foot peaks. We had our sights set on a fourteener: fourteen thousand feet of rocks, trees, views, and thin air. So we set out early one morning to summit Mt. Quandary, the tallest peak of the Ten-Mile Range in the Rocky Mountains.

My brother, a college runner, and I slowly left my dad behind as we rocketed to the top. Though challenging, we crushed that mountain, summiting in just a few hours. The view from the top was, as expected, spectacular. We waited at the top for my dad, and as I lay on my back with my hat over my face, I began to feel an all-too-familiar feeling. Despite being several thousand feet above the tree line, that nauseous pine smell seemed to come rushing back, as if it were grabbing me by the stomach and pulling me down from where I clearly didn't belong. When I stood up to begin the trip down, my legs felt weak, and my head throbbed. I had to get down fast.

Climbing up the mountain was hard, but coming down, the part that was supposed to be my reward for the hard work that was behind me, was sheer misery. I was in excellent shape, but my lungs couldn't seem to hold enough of that thin air. On the way up, I was sure-footed and strong. On the way down, I tripped, stumbled, and fell, carried by legs that couldn't hold me and lungs that felt completely insufficient. I left behind on that mountainside three solid piles of half-digested trail mix, for which I'm sure the chipmunks were grateful.

To top it all off, the thin atmosphere and the relentless alpine sun so burned my face that the next day my lips were so blistered and swollen that I could barely open my mouth wide enough to bite into the burger I had for lunch. You might have thought I'd attempted Everest by how I looked. My brother and my dad, of course, were just fine.

So yes, I'm unbreakable. Unsinkable. Just like the *Titanic*. I've climbed to the top of many mountains and looked down at the view my success has afforded me. I've looked down at those struggling behind me, feeling superior and prideful. But on that mountaintop, my journey wasn't over. And though I arrived at the top from a place of strength, summiting well before others, I couldn't linger there. My body wouldn't allow it. I had to lean on my brother and my father the whole way down.

I've often felt tempted to look down on those I thought were weak, brushing them off as weak-minded with no willpower or no discipline. It's easy to look down from a position of strength and confidence and judge those who don't share your same strengths. It's easy for me anyway. But I've learned that there are limits to my strength, and there are limits to yours too. We are all incredibly different. Every one of us has a breaking point. Just when you think you're unstoppable, the very same mountain you thought rested firmly beneath your feet will rise up and crush you. It'll leave you struggling, and you'll be forced to lean on the few who were made to withstand it.

We're all broken. We're all flawed. It has taken me some time to truly understand this, not just pay it lip service. I still have to tell my pride to step aside sometimes and take a back seat to compassion and empathy. After all, how many people could have looked at me stumbling down that mountain and, knowing nothing else, thought to themselves, *He surely doesn't belong up here. Why did he attempt this? Clearly he's not strong enough.*

Would they have been right? Maybe. Maybe not. But they didn't see the climb. They didn't see me at my best. They just caught a snapshot of me in my weakness. It's easy to look upon someone in their weakness and see only that, especially if that weakness happens to be your strength. It's a trap we can all fall into.

I think one of the reasons God gave us weaknesses was because it's so easy to judge from our places of strength. And because it's so easy to judge from our places of strength, this is precisely why we feel we must hide our weaknesses. We must hide our struggles and cover up the blisters and burns, lest a stranger—or, worse, a friend—see them and, with a prideful eye, write us off as if we don't belong. So we cover up our wounds with makeup and carry on, posting pictures from the mountaintop. The problem with this is that our weaknesses aren't meant to be hidden. Our struggles aren't meant to be handled alone. "Carry each other's burdens, and in this way you will fulfill the law of Christ" (Galatians 6:2).

Burdens can't be shared if they are hidden. From your place of strength, look without pride on others' weaknesses. From your place of weakness, accept without shame the strength of others.

A shared struggle is a manageable one. A shared struggle turns weakness into strength. But oh, how we resist this. When we look at our phones and scroll, we see strength after strength, mountaintop after mountaintop. Had social media existed when I climbed that mountain, I probably would have shared the picture from the top too. Would I have posted my piles of trail mix or my burned, blistered skin? I don't think so. To post those would be to admit that I struggled, showcasing my weakness. Forget that. Who wants to see that anyway?

So we scroll on and on through the pictures of mountaintops others have climbed and think to ourselves, *Oh, how weak I must be!* We see their strength but feel only our struggles.

Shared struggles? What good is that? This generation—your generation that grew up with social media and no memory of life before it—is the strongest and most independent generation ever. You have perfect teeth, perfect smiles, perfect friends, and perfect lives. You have accomplishment after accomplishment. At least that's the way it appears on Facebook.

Behind the curtain, though, is another story entirely. On the far side of the mountain are vulnerabilities, unrealistic expectations of yourself and others, struggles, weaknesses, anxiety, and insecurity. But God forbid anyone ever sees even the slightest hint of that. Hide them. Disguise them. Cover them up with whatever you can find. Pretend they don't exist.

But you know that your struggles and weaknesses are a part of what makes you human. We connect through them. If we allow ourselves to be vulnerable, we can relate through them. It's time to be real and quit pretending everything is okay. We need each other. In fact, we *need* to need each other. Our burdens are too heavy to carry alone, and the stakes are far too high. No, you don't need to broadcast them to your six thousand friends on social media, but you do need to share them. Share them with your closest friends and your family. I can help you up that mountain if you help me down. You may have a problem you think no one else can help you with or that no one else has struggled with, and it may be true that your friends can't solve it for you, but you'd be surprised to know how much help you'll find just by sharing it. Emotional burdens can still be shared and made lighter. Sometimes just being there, being present, is enough to help someone down the mountain.

Share your struggles. And for heaven's sake, ask for help when you need it. Be a generation that bears one another's burdens, for in so doing, you fulfill the law of Christ.

Epilogue

The other day, I completely lost it. After many nights in a row with too little sleep, dealing with sick children, and coping with all the stress that life likes to pile on us at the most inopportune times, I finally let my temper go. I'd been up half the night, tending to crying babies, when I found myself lying in bed, unable to sleep. I glanced at the clock and saw it was a little before 5:00 a.m. My wife had already left for her morning workout, and I knew there was no going back to sleep for me, so I decided to get up. There was no point in lying there anymore. Plus, maybe I could get a little work done while the house was finally quiet and all the kids were asleep.

I got up, splashed some water on my face, grabbed a cup of coffee, and sat down on the couch with my laptop. I've found that the mornings are the only time I can get any real work done. When the house is quiet and my mind is fresh, I can sit in peace on the couch, hot cup of coffee in hand, and make some progress before the sun comes up. In the evenings, I'm too exhausted to sit down and think about anything. By that time, I've already had a full day's work, come home, answered a thousand questions from my kids (mostly with "not now" or simply "no"), and saved my twin babies from certain death about a dozen times. I'm tapped out after that. I'm running on empty. It's that hour before the sun peeks over my fence, before the house comes alive, that I get my best thinking done.

Or so I thought.

I hadn't sat down for two minutes when I heard one of the

twins begin to cry. Frustrated, I set my computer down and went in their room to see if I could get away with popping a pacifier back in her mouth. Not this time. I held her, patted her, and rocked her, but there was no stemming the flow of tears. She was not going back to sleep. Reluctantly, I carried her to the living room and set her down next to me on the couch. After a few minutes of wallowing all over me and mashing the keys down on my computer, I set her down on the floor. She walked around for a good thirty seconds before deciding the floor was not where she wanted to be. She wobbled back over to me, grabbed my knee, and started whining to be picked up again. This went on for another five minutes until I slammed my computer shut, scooped her back up, carried her back to her room, and placed her in her crib. *I'll settle for crying over this nonsense.*

The whimpering and whining started immediately when I closed her door. *I'll just ignore it.*

For about five minutes, I stared blankly at my computer until I heard a door open, followed by footsteps coming down the hall.

"I can't sleep," said my seven-year-old, standing there in his underwear.

Ahh!

"Can I sleep in your bed?"

"Yes. Fine. Go," I said sharply, which was probably not the tone he was looking for at 5:30 in the morning. It wasn't like anyone was sleeping in my bed anyway. I reached for my coffee, only to find that it was already cold.

Another few minutes went by when the whimpering coming from the twins' room grew into full-on screaming, which naturally woke up her twin sister too. *I can't take this anymore! Can't I just have some peace?!*

Surrendering to the fact that my productive hour would not be at all productive that morning, I once again slammed the computer shut, scooped another baby out of her crib, and carried her through my room, where my wide-awake son lay on my bed with the light on, sure to have a meltdown later that day for not getting enough sleep. I plopped her on the floor of the bathroom to rummage through my drawers and cabinets while I took a shower. I was furious, frustrated, exhausted, overwhelmed, and utterly defeated. And the day was just beginning.

That's when I lost it. While waiting for the water to warm up in the shower, I kicked and threw my clothes around and violently punched the air into submission, silently screaming muffled curse words to myself. I'm sure I looked ridiculous, flailing around, chest billowing like I'd just run a four-minute mile, while one of my sixteen-month-olds no doubt looked on with delight at the spectacle. It was a full-blown tantrum. A man-tantrum. A *mantrum*.

It's embarrassing to admit that I sometimes break down like that, but my point in telling this story is that I'm by no means perfect. Sometimes I'm short-tempered with my wife. I'm impatient with my children. I'm just as susceptible to the vices that technology harbors as anyone else. And while I'm generally quite secure in my own skin, I can still hear the subtle whispers of inadequacy when I see others triumph and I'm reminded of my own shortfalls.

I still get things wrong. I'm unable to live up to my own standards. I struggle on occasion to take my own advice. And yes, I even have a rare *mantrum* every now and then. But the direction contained within these pages is forward-looking. It's about where you are going rather than where you've been. We cannot forget our mistakes; nor can we change them. But we can hold fast to the wisdom of others and let their guidance direct our steps through every challenge that awaits us in the future. Perhaps you've been reading this book and found yourself reflecting on all the times you've gotten things wrong. Maybe you've analyzed every relationship failure you've succumbed to up to this point, wishing you'd done things differently. Looking back to hash out some of your past mistakes is fine for a little while, but you can't linger there. You must choose to move forward, carrying with you the experience and wisdom that came at a price.

This isn't a book to read quickly and toss aside to collect dust on the bookshelf. My hope is that it is one that you will return to as you overcome challenge after challenge. Allow it to be that little reminder you need when you're feeling lost, when you forget who you are, or when you're struggling with relationships or loneliness. Let it whisper truth to you when you find yourself wandering in the desert or, as fortune dictates, when you find yourself planted firmly on the mountaintop. It's a book to be shared, discussed, and wrestled with openly among friends.

When you find yourself wrapped up in the mire of social media, letting picture after picture and post after post dictate how you perceive yourself, I hope you come back to the truth that you are more than your status update and more than the comments left on your wall. You are beautifully and wonderfully made.

I hope you connect with friends and family in a real and personal way, fostering the relationships in front of you at the expense of those on your computer screen and not the other way around.

I hope you protect the weak and stand up for what's right, though it may cost you dearly. I hope you afford yourself the opportunity to be secure in singleness rather than chasing relationship after relationship to find happiness. I hope you find your identity rooted firmly in Christ.

I pray that you guard your heart from the temptations it's so susceptible to and, when it's time, when your heart and mind are in agreement, you find love and fulfillment. I hope you set healthy, realistic expectations of love, sex, and marriage.

I hope you love sacrificially, doing the works of love even when the emotion is lost. I hope you live boldly, inviting failure and allowing it to sharpen your strength and resolve. I hope that, when you err, you do so on the side of generosity, kindness, and grace instead of safety, selfishness, and judgment.

I hope you win more than you lose. But when you lose, I hope you lose with grace. And I pray that when struggles find you, addiction enslaves you, depression weighs you down, or you're struggling to tread water in your marriage, you will refrain from retreating into isolation, but instead ask for help, knowing the truth that a shared struggle is a lighter burden to carry.

This past Christmas, my family and I attended worship together at our church. The Christmas service is one I look forward to all year. I love the lights, the carols, the lit candles, and the green garland peppered with holly. This year, when I looked down the row, I saw that it was almost entirely occupied by my family: my wife, my parents, and my brothers and their families. Even though I held a wiggling, sick baby through the service, I couldn't help but be overwhelmed with gratitude at the opportunity to worship together with my family. If you knew the struggles we'd been through over the past twelve months, then you'd know what a precious moment this was, how different it could have been.

It was a special moment, and while we were sitting there together, the promises of grace never seemed more tangible. Christmas is the celebration of what has transpired and the hope of what's to come. It's a reminder that God is always with us and His grace covers a million failures.

You will fall short. You will struggle. But take comfort because, when the dust settles, the God of hope is ready to shower you with grace upon grace. And when the weight of the world is on your shoulders, know that this too will pass and someday you will find yourself seated in a row or around a table with your family and your loved ones. And that moment will mean more to you than it ever has before.

Author's Note

You made it! Wow, good job! If you enjoyed this book, I'll ask you to go one step further. Please leave me a review on Amazon or wherever you purchased this book. Your honest feedback would be greatly appreciated and help to inform my future projects. You can also find me on my website, www.JoelBennettBooks.com, or send me an email at Joel@JoelBennettBooks.com. Thank you so much for reading!

CPSIA information can be obtained
at www.ICGtesting.com
Printed in the USA
LVHW09s0958290818
588502LV00001B/10/P